For You

WHAT HIGHLY EF

PEOP
DON'T
TELL YO

Published by
TRUTHFUL BOOKS
St. Veitgasse 6
1130 Vienna
Austria

ISBN 978-3-200-03645-1

Edited by Dorine Jennette
Final edit by Mark Bilbrey
Executive Producer: Bernhard Einsiedler
Script Consultant: Fabian Eder
Social Media Support: Lyndsi Stafford, eLuminate Marketing
Production Support: Stefan Moser, Aumayer Digital Publishing

"This book is like a breath of fresh air amongst other management books. The beautifully designed graphic novel format allows for messages without words, which adds a powerful dimension. The book offers a leadership experience for everybody 'looking for answers.' A great and recommended read for busy managers who hardly give themselves the time to stop and think about where they are now and want to be next."

Reggy de Feniks, Managing Partner, 9senses,
Barcelona, Spain (www.9senses.com),
coauthor of Reinventing Financial Services and
Reinventing Customer Engagement,
co-founder DIA (www.digitalinsuranceagenda.com)

"I think this story will touch a nerve with modern managers. It is current in its focus on 'values' versus 'greed/money/status' and at the same time it touches the timeless theme of 'the search for oneself.' A super-inspiring story. I was personally touched by it. I like the overall message and the combination of rich dialogue and vivid images that really makes the story come to life."

Arne Arens, Global Brand President, The North Face,
San Francisco, CA, USA (www.thenorthface.com)

"What happens when a life-changing experiences breaks a man and his cherished mythology wide open? Madhu takes us on a phantasmagoric journey which chronicles this experience with such psychological acuity that it throws a mirror to our own lives and the questions we have been evading all the while. The business world, long used to monotonous rhymes of leadership myths past their expiry date, badly needs to hear the story of John Myers."

Venkataraman Ramachandran, Storyteller and Consultant,
Hyderabad, India (www.linkedin.com/in/venkinesis)

"Many of the management principles learnt at graduate school don't apply anymore. Young managers and promising talents don't shape their careers along traditional patterns. Money or power aren't the only measurements of success. They search for true happiness and fulfillment in their lives. Madhu Einsiedler and Gerald Hartwig have excellently carved out this quest of deeper meaning. The story and the way it is characterized in words and visuals is surely an eye-opener and inspiration for many executives and talents aiming for the top job."

Edgar C. Britschgi Wang, Chairman, Combo Management
Visiting Professor MIM-Kyiv and GMBA,
Taipei, Taiwan (www.combo-management.com)

"A business book in a refreshing style (and I'm not into comics at all!) – fast like a race-car, fun to read and great food for thought."

Stefan Holzer, Business Director Intl, Medtronic
(www.medtronic.com)

"Madhu has done two remarkable things: She has realized the power of graphic storytelling as a medium to convey ideas in ways that the customary management book cannot; and she has harnessed that realization to the simple but powerful story of how discovering who we truly are as human beings can give us the insights to better manage projects and lead people."

Robin Todd, Technical Program Manager, Amazon Lumberyard,
Austin, TX, USA

"In some moments I've thought, "This is my husband!" I believe managers will enjoy it and will find inspiration for professional and personal growth. I would love John and Margret to come back in a second volume."

Renata Sir, Accountant, IT Methods,
Brussels, Belgium

"Madhu Einsiedler has weaved an amazing story and has shown us how we entangle ourselves. I have been concerned and passionate about unlocking an individual's infinite potential. Madhu has brought attention to the varied masks (in all their glory) we cloud ourselves with – which is probably the biggest road block in our progress to satisfaction and fulfillment. Thank you, Madhu, for showing us a way to holistically accept and compassionately understand our lives."

Chakradhar Iyyunni, Faculty, Larson & Toubro Institute of Project Management
Vadodara, Gujarat, India
(www.researchgate.net/profile/Chakradhar_Iyyunni;
www.linkedin.com/in/ciyyunni/)

"An invaluable read for both managers and employees alike! Recognizing the influence of external expectations, and how they mold us into someone unlike our true self, is so vital for defining our own work/life harmony.
Being invited to join John on his self-discovery allowed me to self-reflect at every one of his decision points. The powerful emotions, so effectively conveyed in the images, challenged me to empathize and evaluate my own honest reactions to each situation."

Martine Lewis, eCommerce Business Analyst; Thinkwrap Commerce,
Ottawa, Canada (www.thinkwrap.com

"Managers out there! Are you struggling to find answers for how to solve challenges at work or maybe with your loved ones? This book will certainly not give you answers on that. Sorry. What this book can do for you is to inspire and awaken the inspirational leader in you. It is an innovative, whole new concept in managers' rejuvenation. If this book doesn't make you start doing things differently or confirm that some things you do in your life are the right ones, no book will."

Franjo Hanzl, Director, Global Alliance Management, Orexigen Therapeutics,
Croatia (www.orexigen.com)

"I believe those managers who are not only on the quest for more status and money, but want to find their own way of true leadership, will love this book and benefit from it tremendously. I read the story with enthusiasm and, for me, it was what a good read should be – emotional, intriguing, intellectually satisfying, and long-lasting. The character of John Myers mirrored myself, and again and again I felt like I was reading my own story. The character of the hermit is like the internal wisdom every leader strives for, the personalization of the internal true leader."

Wilhelm Hofmann, CEO, SEW-Eurodrive GmbH,
Vienna, Austria (www.sew-eurodrive.at)

"Madhu uses high-impact language on wise lessons of life. At times, the book gives me tough confrontations with my self-built mental prisons. The process between the hermit and John Myers often leaves me silently smiling and gives me language to address the issues that come along with the rat race I and people in the world around me are in."

Katharina Schmidt, CEO/Founder, Inspiration & Discipline,
Amsterdam, Netherlands/ San Francisco, CA, USA
(www.inspirationanddiscipline.com)

"This book is an awesome story of human development, love and respect, but also much more. The story itself, and the way the story is told, touched me deeply and initiated a sustainable process of personal reflection and even growth. This book shall become a bible for those on the road of self-discovery."

Richard Huebner, Co-founder, Dignit Consulting,
Vienna, Austria (www.dignit.at)

WHAT HIGHLY EFFECTIVE PEOPLE DON'T TELL YOU

Madhu Einsiedler
Writer

Gerald Hartwig
Artist

PREFACE

I have been working for more than twenty years as a leadership coach and consultant for organizational and personal change. If you asked me about the most important lesson I've learned, I'd say this: change and transformation are two fundamentally different things.

Over the last twenty years, I changed jobs, countries, clients, partners, apartments (at one point I had four different apartments in three different countries). I learned and changed methods and techniques. I worked my way through a lot of the must-reads on self-improvement. I thrived on becoming a better manager, leader, coach, consultant, and human being.

Every change was exciting. As each project challenged me, I learned new skills and developed new behaviors. I felt like I was growing.

Yet, what I saw each morning in the mirror was the same face. And after each exciting change, something old and familiar settled in, an unease, a pale taste, like a fading memory of a bad dream that lingers, yet we can't articulate it.

I've seen a similar pattern in organizations and clients I worked with.

We change and yet, on a fundamental level, we stay the same. We change job titles, earn more money, are more productive, learn different skills, get a bigger house, a new partner. On an organizational level it's one change initiative after the other. Change is about going higher, faster, increasing revenue, reducing costs.

Change keeps us busy. It's like change is an end in itself.

And it might well be. It makes us believe we grow.

Change is like acquiring and putting on different glasses. We are proud of all the many glasses we have collected. We showcase them.

Transformation, however, is quite a different game. Transformation is to see with different eyes.

Transformation changes who we are. It's a deep and personal process. We face our self-deceptions. Illusions and beliefs that kept us safe and warm dissolve. We struggle. We fall. It's often painful. When we get up, something fundamental is different.

A personal transformation of that nature is not the usual story you might hear. It's not easily shared.

Enter John Myers, the protagonist of this book.

He's of course a fictional character. Yet he's based on my extensive experience supporting and accompanying people from different backgrounds, nationalities, occupations, and personalities on their unique quest for success and growth.

May John's story inspire and inform your own journey from mere change to true transformation.

"I will meet you there."

Rumi

IF YOU ASK ME TO GIVE YOU THE MANAGEMENT SUMMARY OF THIS STORY, I WILL HAVE TO TELL YOU: I DON'T HAVE ONE.

I KNOW - DOESN'T SOUND LIKE A MANAGER AT ALL.

THIS STORY IS NOT SO MUCH ABOUT MANAGEMENT AS IT IS ABOUT ME. I DON'T KNOW ABOUT YOU, BUT I HAVE NEVER LEARNED TO LOOK AT MYSELF WITH THE SAME SCRUTINY AS I LOOK AT BUSINESS.

THE NUMBERS, THE STRATEGY, THE MARKET, THE EMPLOYEES - I LOOK AT THESE OBJECTIVELY, WITHOUT EMOTIONS: I ANALYZE, ASSESS, DECIDE, SET GOALS, EXECUTE, CONTROL.

WHEN IT COMES TO MYSELF - WELL, IT'S OTHER PEOPLE WHO ARE DIFFICULT. THEN AGAIN, IT SEEMS I'M A MASTER OF SELF-DECEPTION.

SURE, I CAN PLAY THE GAME: I HAVE A PERSONAL DEVELOPMENT PLAN, A COACH. I AM PERCEIVED AS FLEXIBLE, EAGER TO LEARN, TO GROW. I HONESTLY THOUGHT I KNEW MY DIFFERENT FACES AND KNEW HOW TO OPERATE THEM AS NEEDED TO REACH MY GOALS. I HONESTLY THOUGHT I WAS IN CONTROL.

AND ISN'T IT ALL ABOUT CONTROL? CONTROL OVER DESTINY, SUCCESS. OR IS IT ABOUT LOVE? ONLY WHEN I PROVE MY WORTH TO THE WORLD WILL I FEEL SAFE AND FINALLY LOVED. WHAT A CLICHÉ.

MAYBE, IF YOU KEPT INSISTING ON A SUMMARY, I'D SAY THIS: LIFE HAS A LIFE OF ITS OWN. IT CANNOT BE CONTROLLED, CANNOT BE MANAGED. AND I'VE ONLY STARTED TO GET TO KNOW WHO I AM.

BUT I'M GETTING AHEAD OF MYSELF.

LET ME START WITH A PROPER INTRODUCTION:

I'M JOHN MYERS.

11

EVERYONE CALLS ME JACK.

 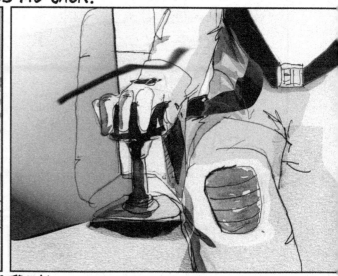

THIS IS MY STORY.

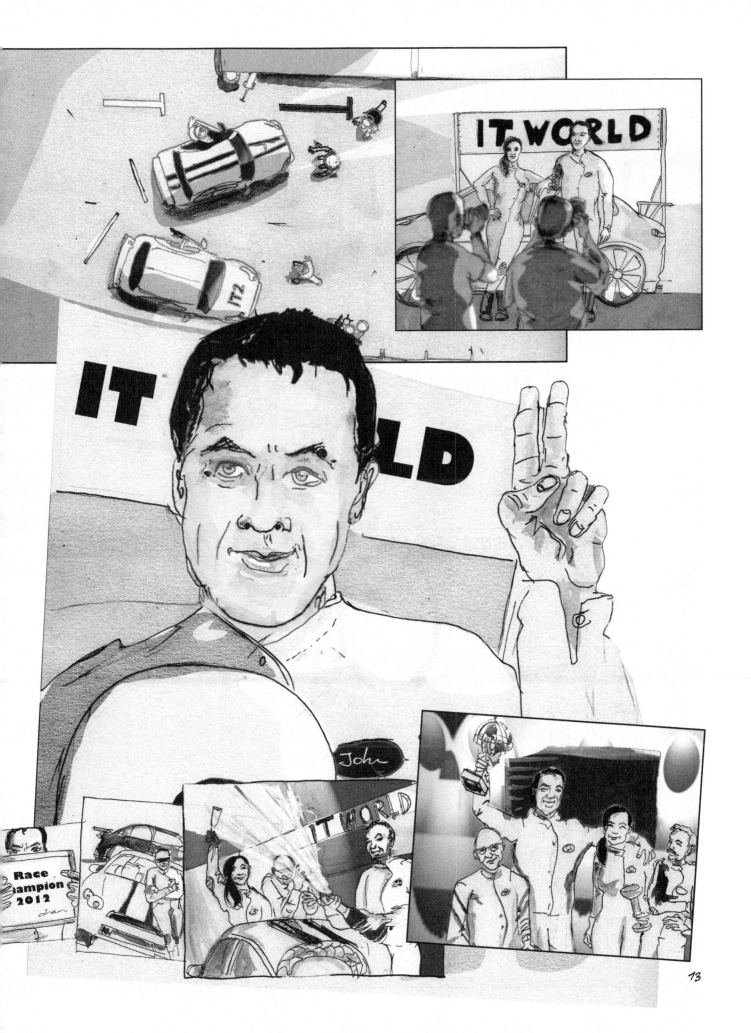

VERY FEW THINGS GAVE ME A KICK LIKE SPEED AND SUCCESS.

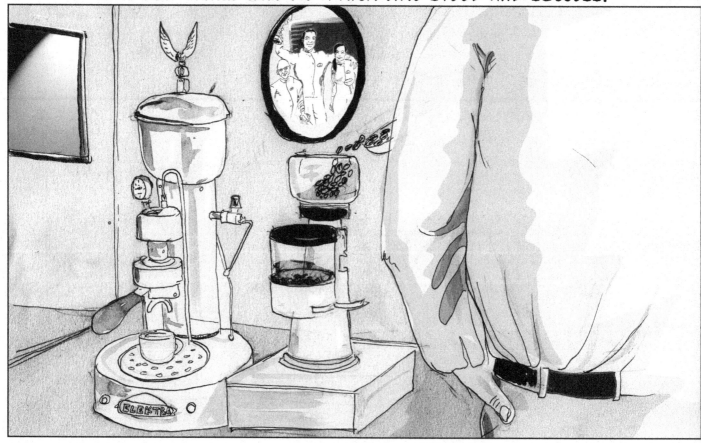

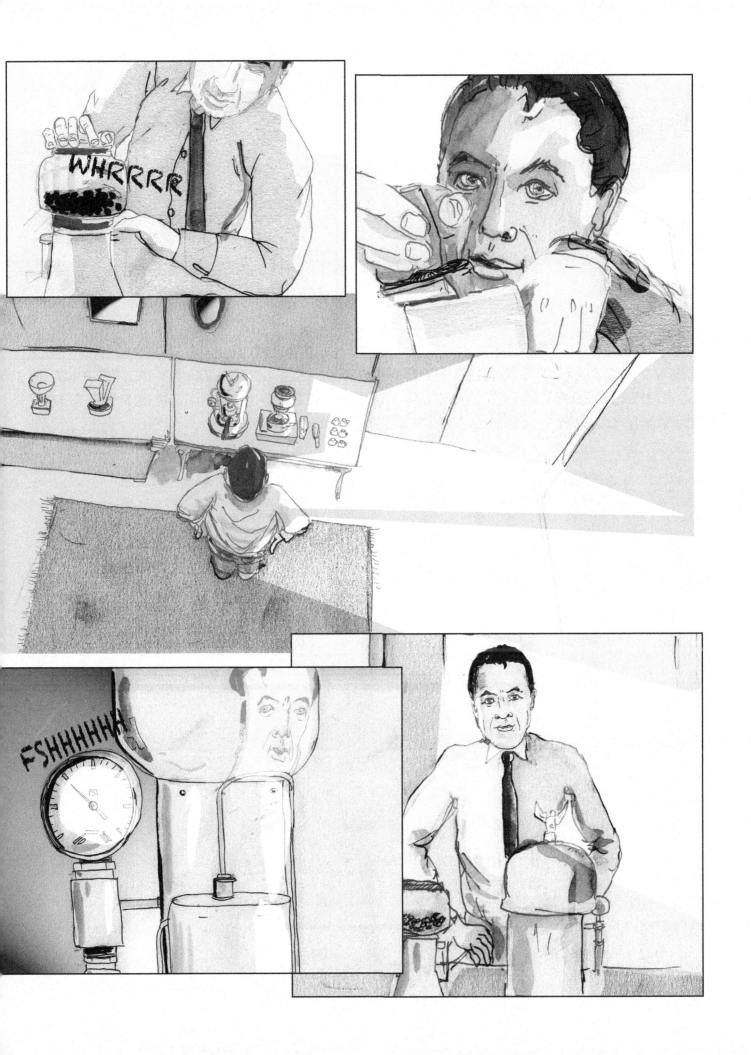

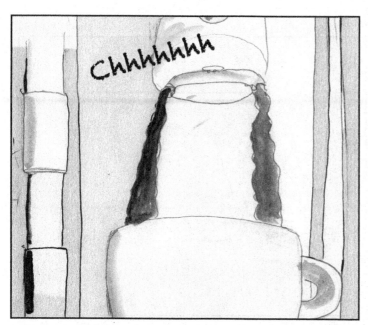

THEN THERE WAS OF COURSE MY FAMILY. GUESS I LOVED FAMILY QUITE A LOT - I GOT MYSELF SEVERAL. AT THE TIME OF THIS STORY, I WAS A FATHER OF THREE WONDERFUL GIRLS, EX-HUSBAND OF TWO LUCKY WOMEN.

MARGRET, MY THIRD WIFE, HAD JUST GIVEN BIRTH TO JOHN-JOHN, MY FIRST SON.

YOU CAN ONLY IMAGINE HOW PROUD I WAS.

THEN THERE WAS CHANG. CHANG AND I, WE WENT BACK A LONG TIME. I TRUSTED HI[

OUR PLANT IN CHINA PROVED THAT HUMANE WORKING CONDITIONS AND HAPPY WALLSTREET ANALYSTS AREN'T MUTUALLY EXCLUSIVE. IN FACT, THEY'RE A GREAT MATCH. OUR NUMBERS WERE QUITE CONVINCING.

CHANG RAN THE PLANT, I BROUGHT MONEY AND CONNECTIONS. I WAS CEO OF TECHTIMES.

THE PLAN WAS, WITHIN 5 YEARS, WE'D MAKE OUR PROCESSES THE INDUSTRY STANDARD.
I WAS ABOUT TO BECOME CEO OF ITWORLD, THE MOTHER COMPANY AND THE BIGGEST PLAYER IN OUR FIELD.

WAAHAAHH

HAVE TO GO ...

GIVE JOHN-JOHN A ...

... KISS.

20

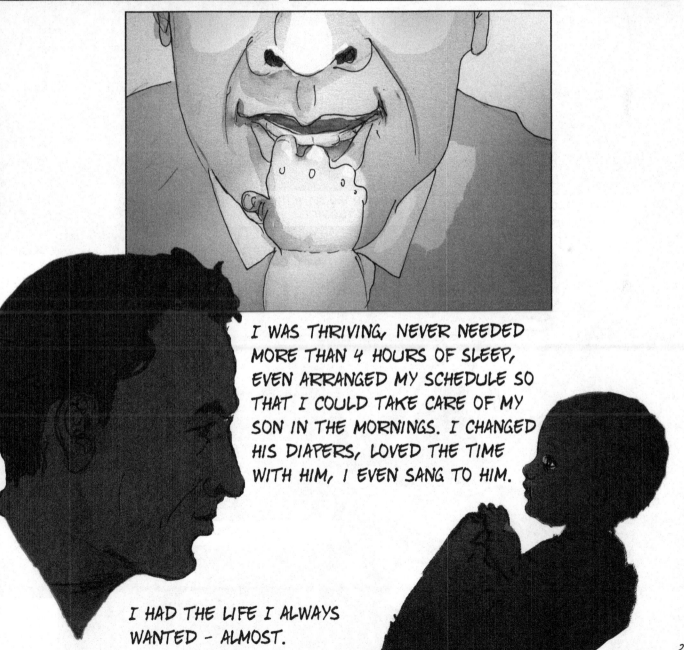

I WAS THRIVING, NEVER NEEDED MORE THAN 4 HOURS OF SLEEP, EVEN ARRANGED MY SCHEDULE SO THAT I COULD TAKE CARE OF MY SON IN THE MORNINGS. I CHANGED HIS DIAPERS, LOVED THE TIME WITH HIM, I EVEN SANG TO HIM.

I HAD THE LIFE I ALWAYS WANTED - ALMOST.

MY FATHER WAS NEVER A MAN EASY TO SATISFY.

BUSINESS PEOPLE SPOKE HIS NAME WITH AW

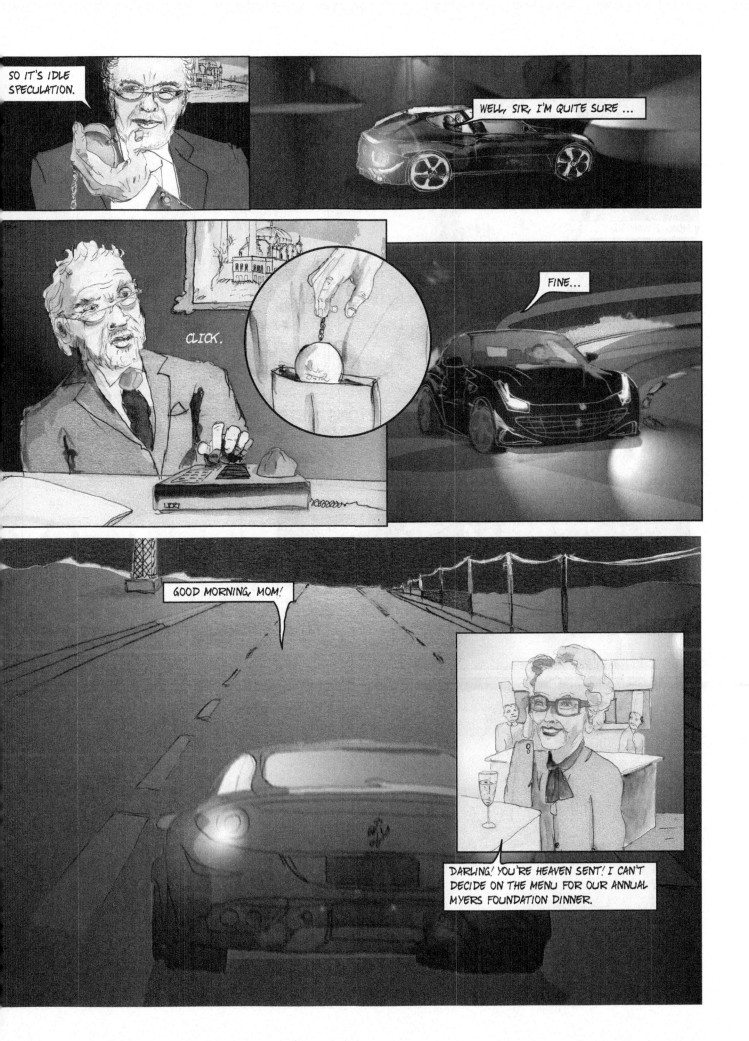

MOM, I WANTED ...

SHOULD I GO FOR THE MEDITERRANEAN VARIATION, ALTHOUGH YOUR FATHER IS NOT A FAN OF IT, BUT IT'S LIGHT AND WE ALL EAT TOO MUCH. BUT DARLING, WHAT DO YOU PREFER? YOU HAVE TO MAKE THE DECISION FOR ME, SWEETHEART, YOU KNOW HOW THOSE THINGS STRESS ME.

MOM'S CHARITY FUNCTIONS WERE LEGENDARY.

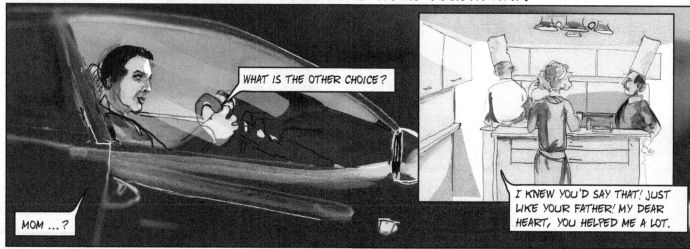

WHAT IS THE OTHER CHOICE?

MOM ...?

I KNEW YOU'D SAY THAT! JUST LIKE YOUR FATHER! MY DEAR HEART, YOU HELPED ME A LOT.

CLICK.

LOVE YOU TOO, MOM.

SUCCESS WAS PART OF MY MAKE-UP. I HAD IT IN MY GENES.

YOU KNOW THOSE MOMENTS
WHEN YOU FEEL INVINCIBLE.

WHEN EVEN THE LACK OF GOOD COFFEE CAN'T ANNOY YOU.

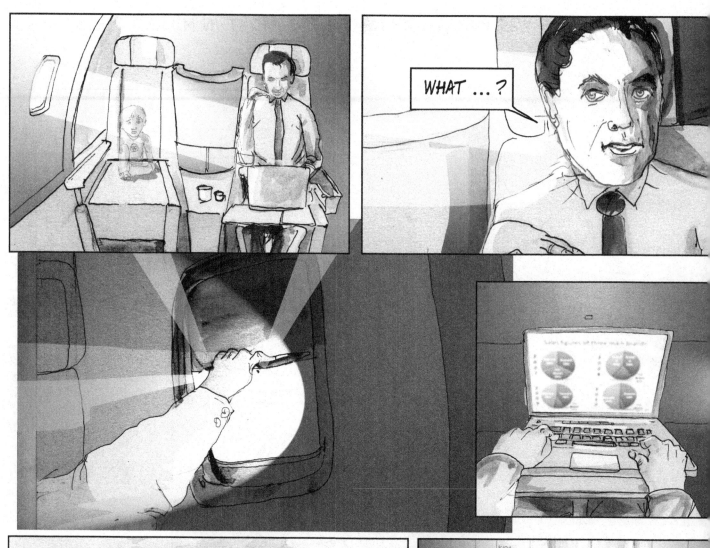

WHAT ... ?

SORRY FOR BEING LATE, JACK. AS I'M SURE HE HAS ALREADY TOLD YOU, WE'RE NOT ABLE TO PROMOTE YOU THIS YEAR. SHAREHOLDERS ARE NERVOUS.

HE HASN'T.

OH, YOU KNOW HIM.

RIING

I HAVE TO ANSWER THIS, JACK.

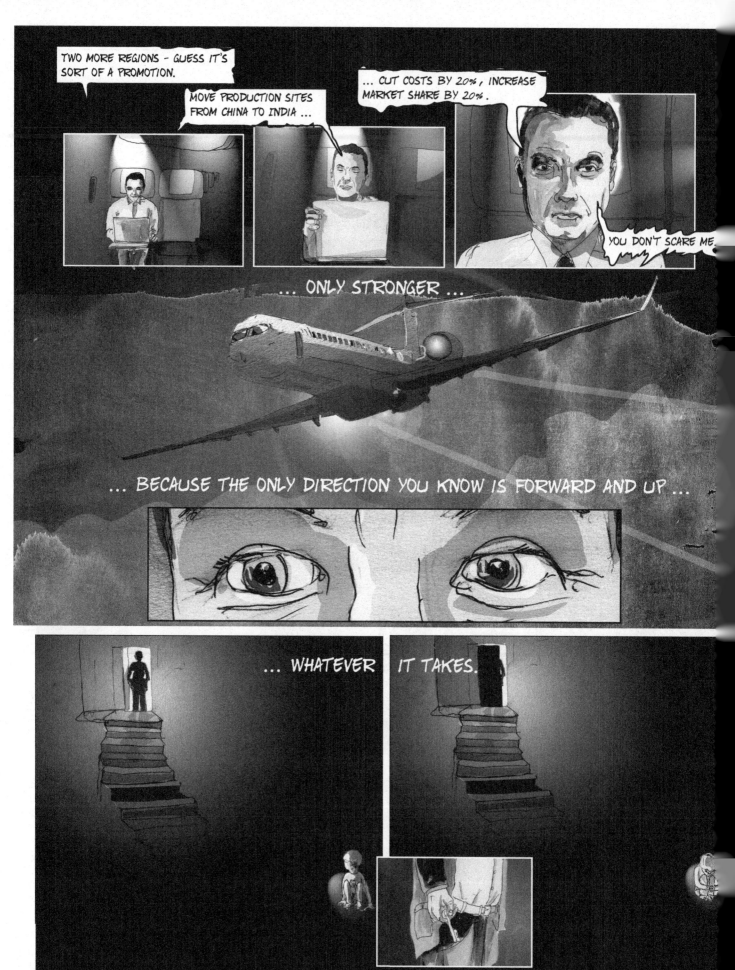

TIM, CFO OF TECHTIMES, AND KATHLEEN, HIS RIGHT HAND, WERE MY INNER MANAGEMENT CIRCLE.

KATHLEEN WAS MY RIGHT HAND, TOO, SO TO SPEAK.

THERE WERE MOMENTS WHEN SHE WANTED MORE, BUT EVENTUALLY SHE WOULD COME TO HER SENSES AGAIN.

WE WERE THE PERFECT MATCH - WE BOTH DROVE ON POWER AND ADRENALINE, WE BOTH TALKED AND MEANT BUSINESS.

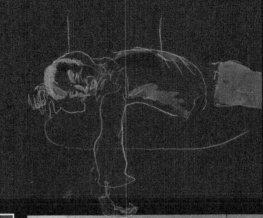

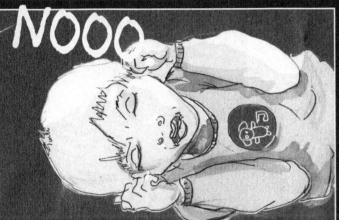

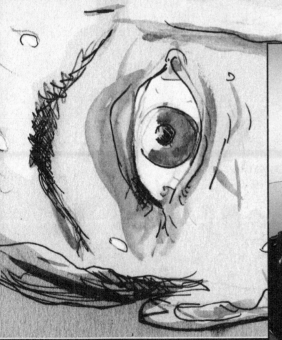

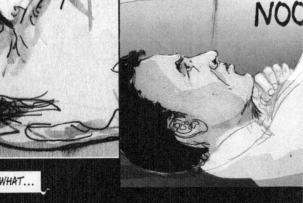

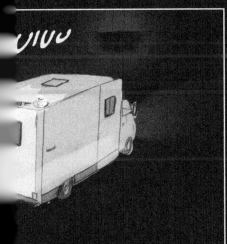

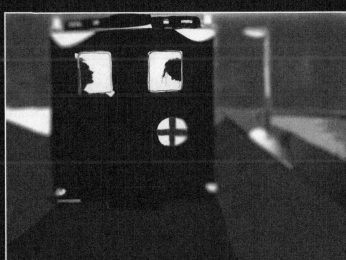

37

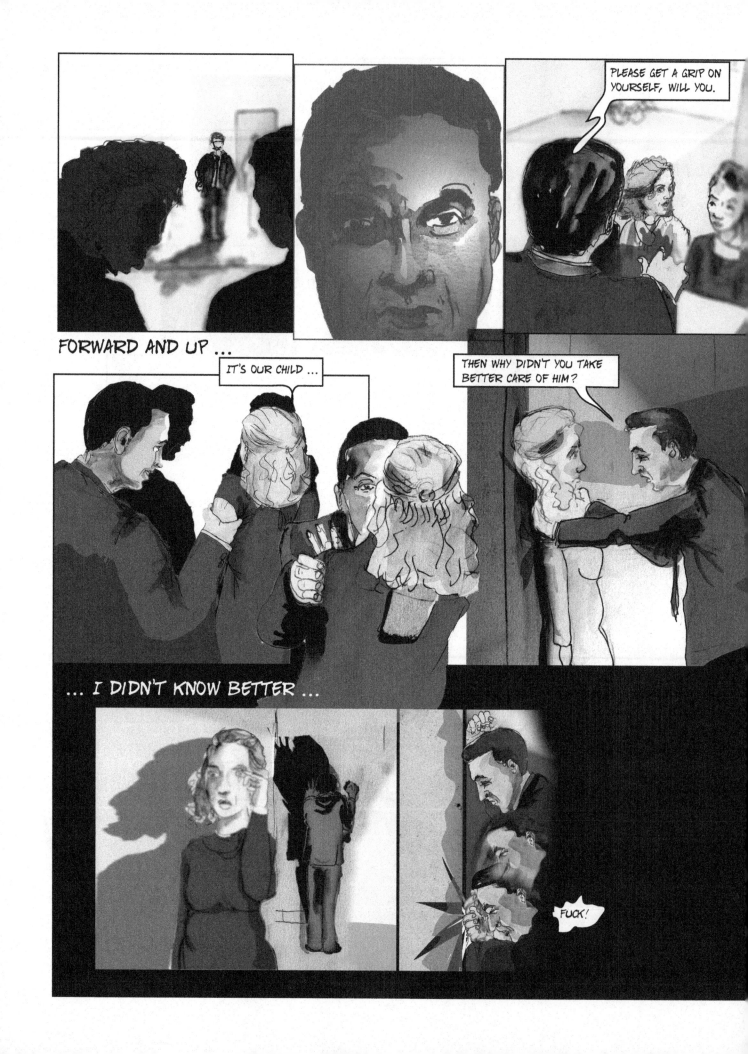

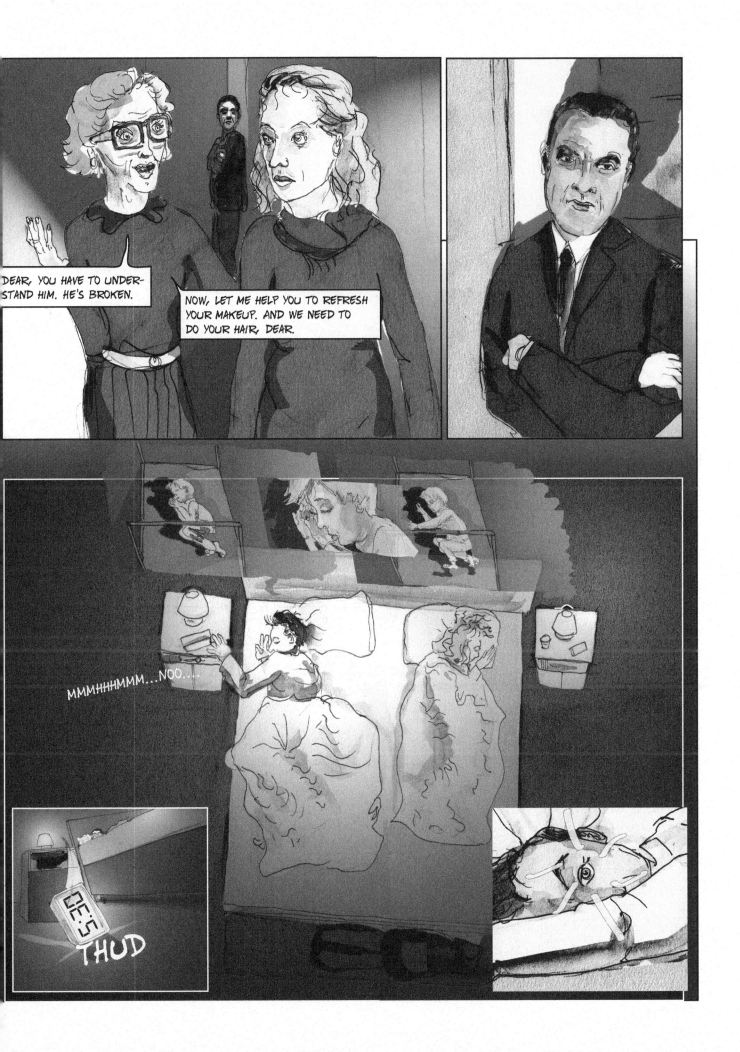

I'M SORRY, SWEETHEART.

HUNGRY MY LITTLE CUTIE, HMM?

FORWARD AND UP – THE ONLY DIRECTION I KNEW, THE ONLY POSSIBLE PATH.

YOU HAVE TO UNDERSTAND ... THE PRESSURE IS IMMENSE ... TWO NEW REGIONS, TEN NEW COUNTRY HEADS ... TIM CAN'T DO THIS BY HIMSELF.

BUT I CAN?

CHANG'S HERE ... MY MOM IS...

YOU AREN'T.

I MADE YOU COFFEE.

I'LL CALL YOU FIRST THING WHEN I ARRIVE.

I'LL CALL YOU AS SOON AS I CAN.

YOU'RE CRAZY, JOHN.

THE SITUATION IS, TIM'S CHECKING WITH LEGAL TO CANCEL ALL CONT- RACTS WITH OUR PRODUCTION PLANT. INDIA IS MORE COST EFFICIENT.

TECHTIMES IS OUR ONLY CLIENT ...

I KNOW THAT, CHANG. I ALSO KNOW THAT ALL YOUR MONEY AND MINE IS INVESTED IN OUR PRODUCTION PLANT.

YOU HAVE BEEN THROUGH A LOT.

I'M DOING EVERYTHING I CAN.

THAT'S THE POINT. YOU CAN'T DO EVERYTHING.

DO YOU REMEMBER HOW WE WANTED TO CHANGE THE WORLD?

YOU NEED TO TAKE A BREAK.

SEEMS LIKE A LIFETIME AGO.

WE NEED PROOF THAT WE CAN COMPETE WITH INDIA, THAT A SOCIALLY RESPONSIBLE PRO- DUCTION SITE IS COMPETITIVE.

I'LL PUT MY TEAM ON IT, BUT YOU ...

DO IT FAST. I'LL HANDLE TIM. AND ... PLEASE ... TAKE CARE OF MARGRET WHILE I'M GONE. SHE'S SO FRAGILE.

CLICK

JACK ...?

LATER THAT EVENING.

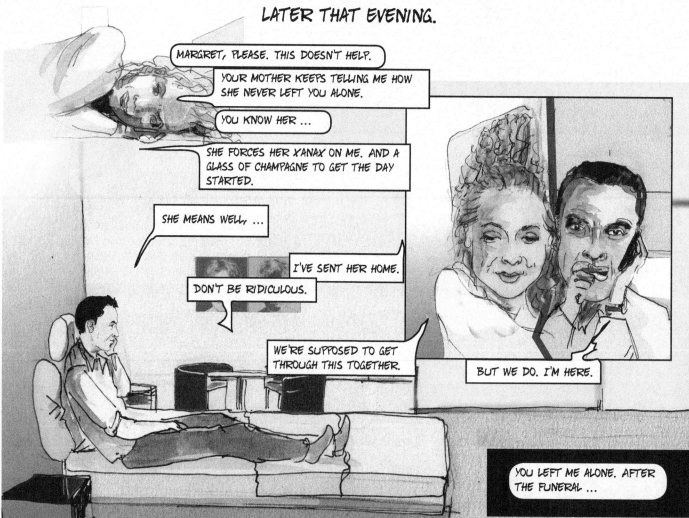

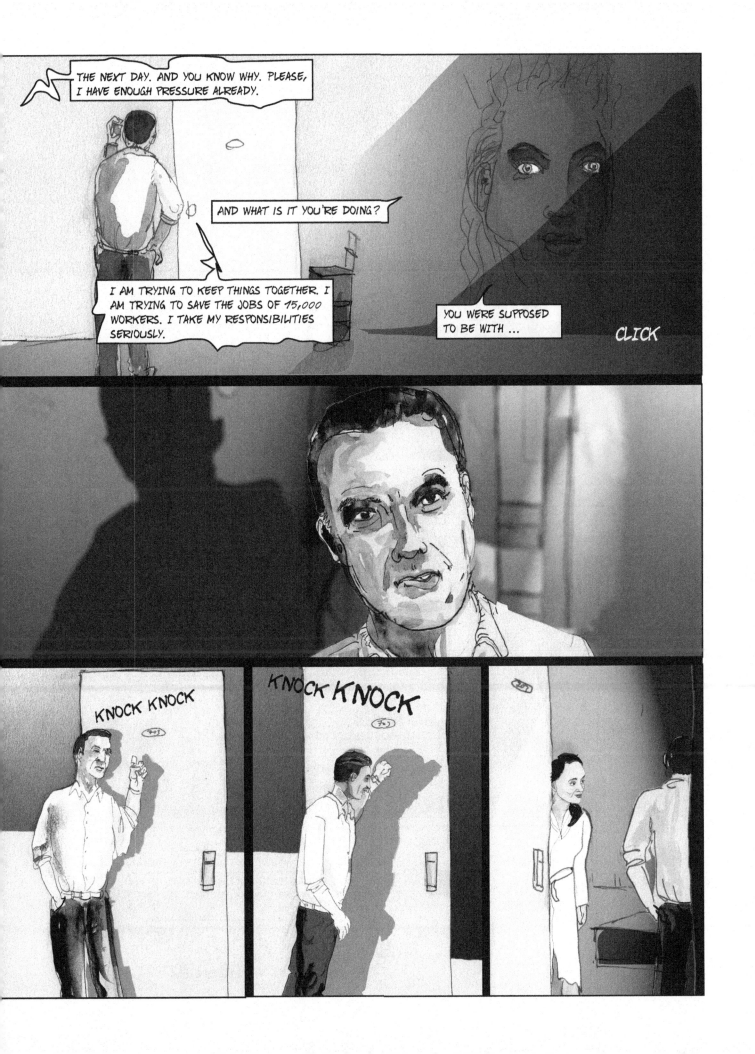

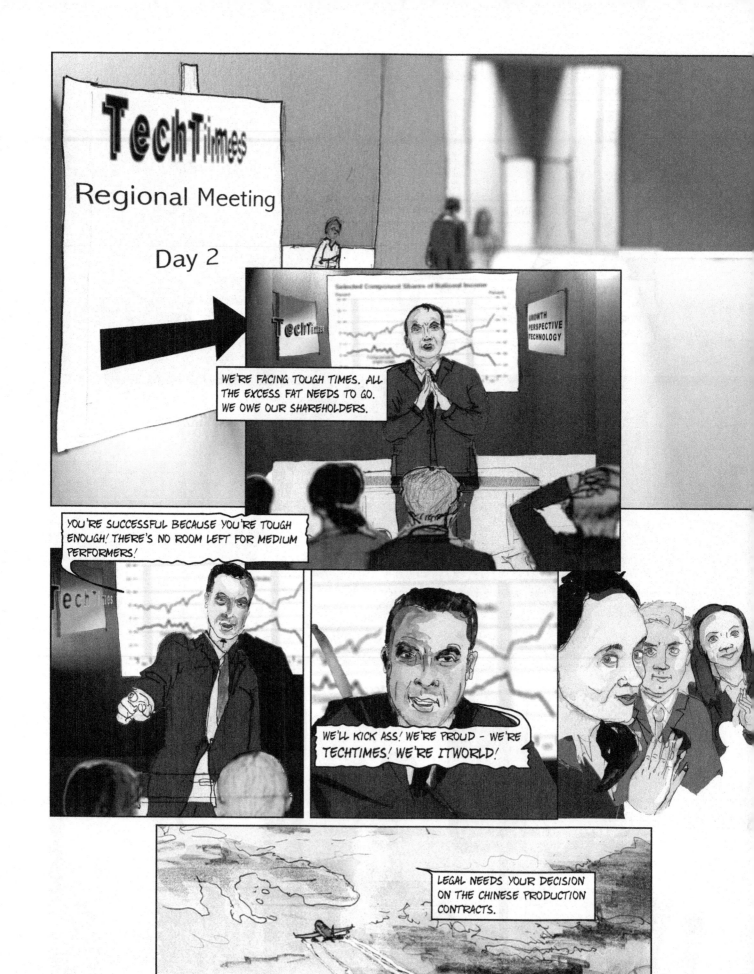

I DON'T AGREE WITH HQ, TIM. CLIENTS ARE SENSITIVE TO WORKING CONDITIONS. THESE ARE ALSO COSTS WE NEED TO TAKE INTO ACCOUNT.

IT'S A PITY, CHANG DID A REAL GOOD JOB. BUT HQ IS PRETTY STRAIGHT FORWARD ON THIS ONE.

YOU'RE A CRAZY IDEALIST.

YOU KNOW I WANT TO MAKE THIS WAY OF PRODUCING AN ITWORLD GUIDELINE.

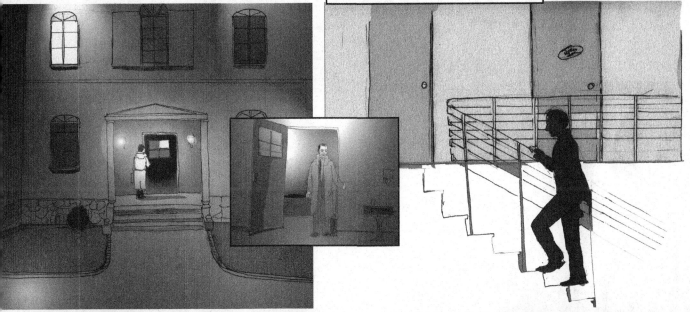

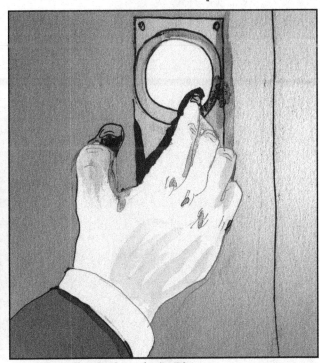

I HAD TO BE STRONG.

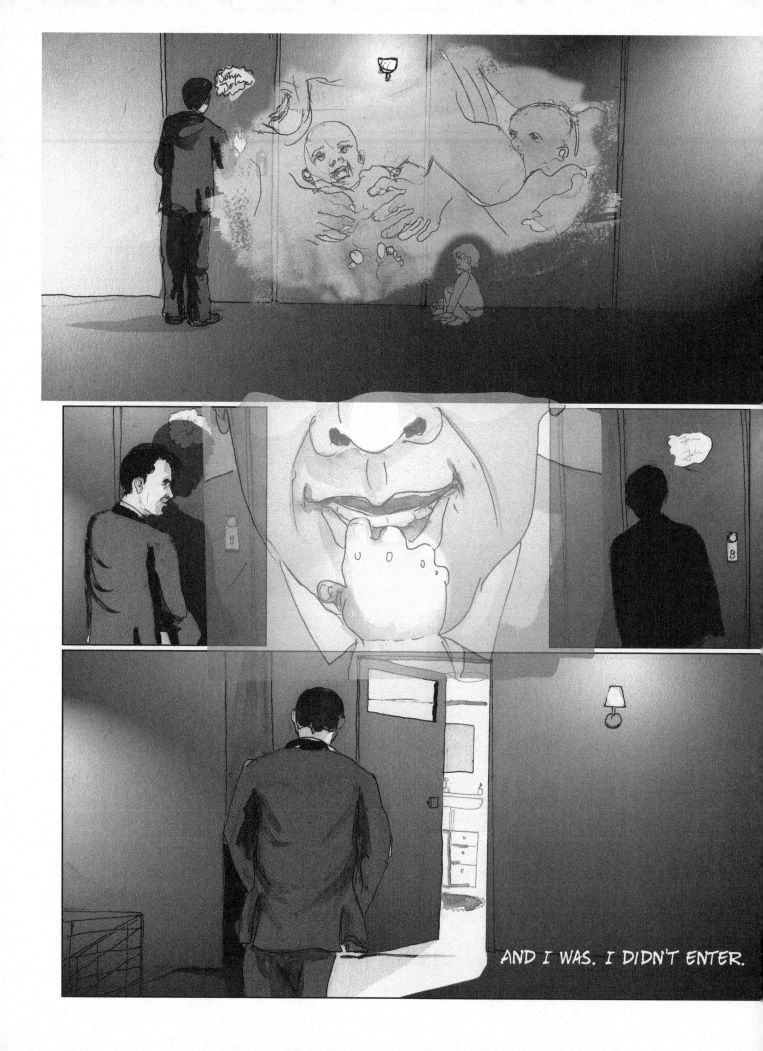

AND I WAS. I DIDN'T ENTER.

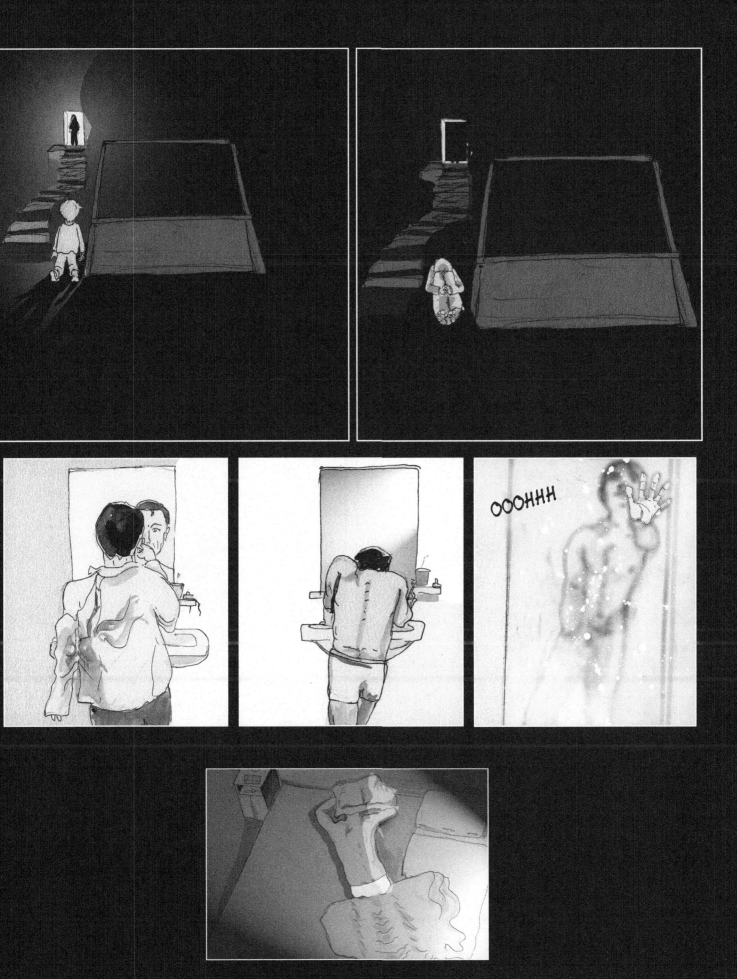

I FELL IN LOVE WITH MARGRET BECAUSE SHE WAS SO DIFFERENT. HER WAY OF LOOKING AT THE WORLD FASCINATED ME. SHE WAS LIKE A CHILD ...

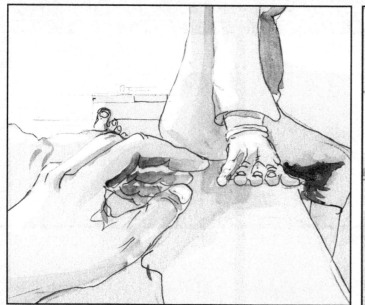

... SURPRISING ...

... EMOTIONAL ...

... IRRATIONAL.

WHEN WE MET, I WAS ON A BUSINESS TRIP, SHE WAS HITCHHIKING. I TOOK HER ALONG.

THE REST OF THE TRIP SHE STAYED WITH ME. THIS WAS THE FIRST TIME I EVER SKIPPED MEETINGS.

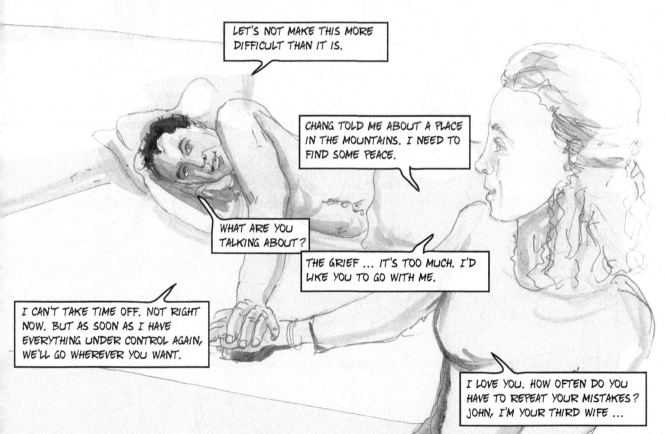

LET'S NOT MAKE THIS MORE DIFFICULT THAN IT IS.

CHANG TOLD ME ABOUT A PLACE IN THE MOUNTAINS. I NEED TO FIND SOME PEACE.

WHAT ARE YOU TALKING ABOUT?

THE GRIEF ... IT'S TOO MUCH. I'D LIKE YOU TO GO WITH ME.

I CAN'T TAKE TIME OFF. NOT RIGHT NOW. BUT AS SOON AS I HAVE EVERYTHING UNDER CONTROL AGAIN, WE'LL GO WHEREVER YOU WANT.

I LOVE YOU. HOW OFTEN DO YOU HAVE TO REPEAT YOUR MISTAKES? JOHN, I'M YOUR THIRD WIFE ...

51

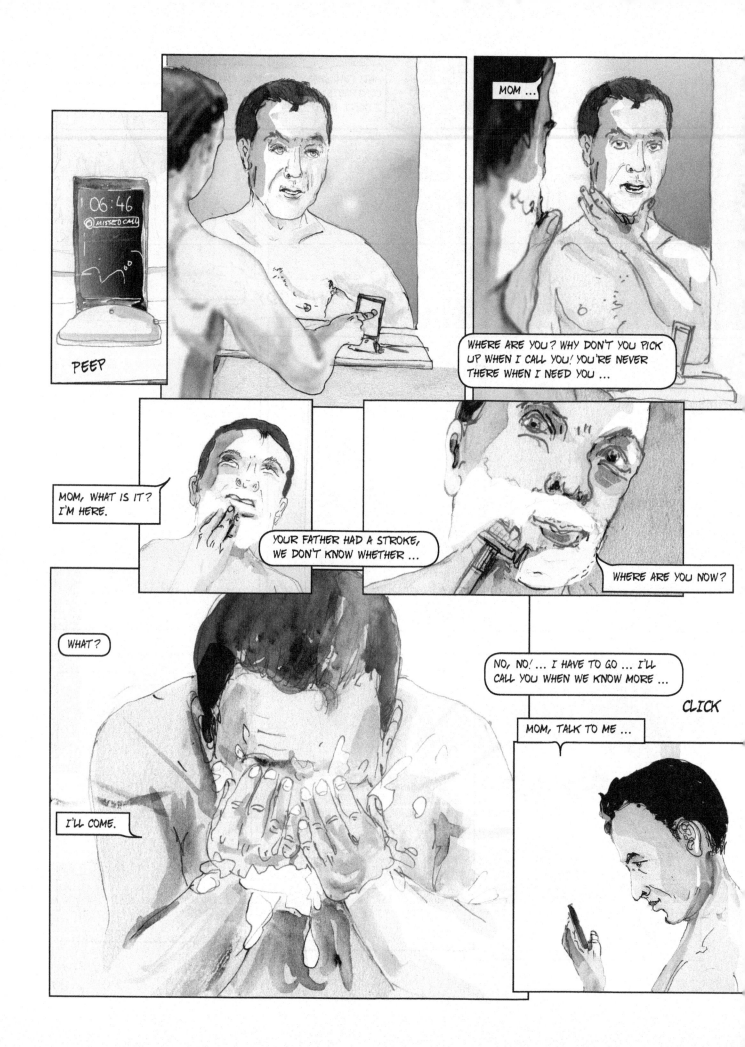

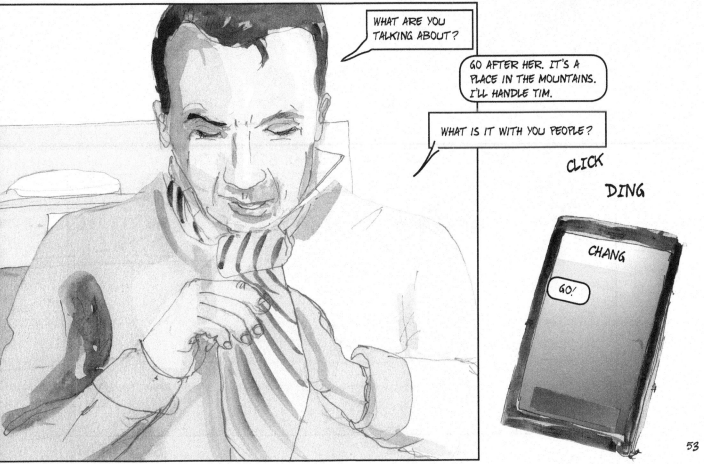

THE PATH LOOKED FORWARD AND UP ...

... AND MARGRET NEEDED MY STRENGTH ...

... SO I WENT.

THE TOP LOOKED DIFFERENT THAN I EXPECTED.

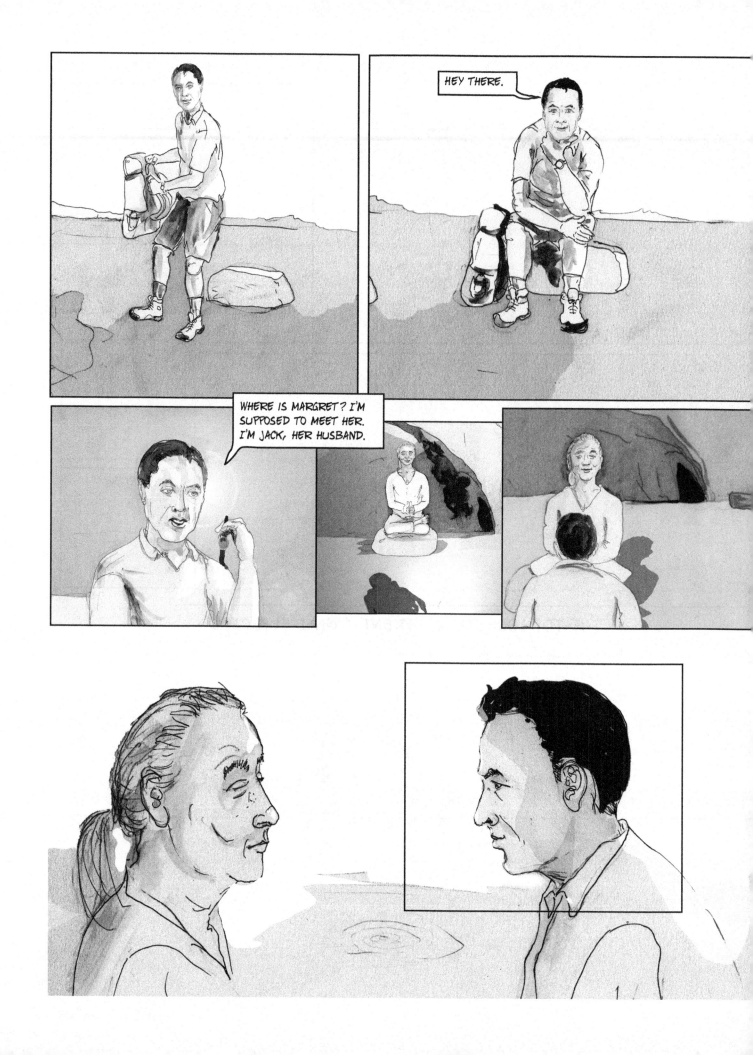

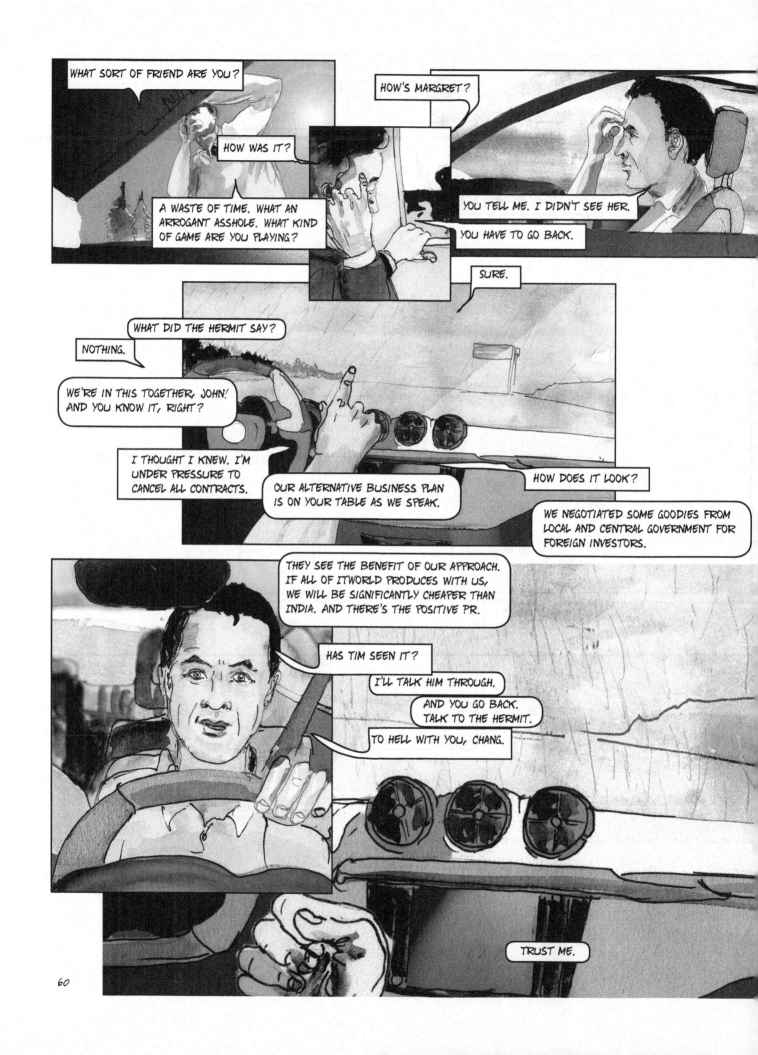

60

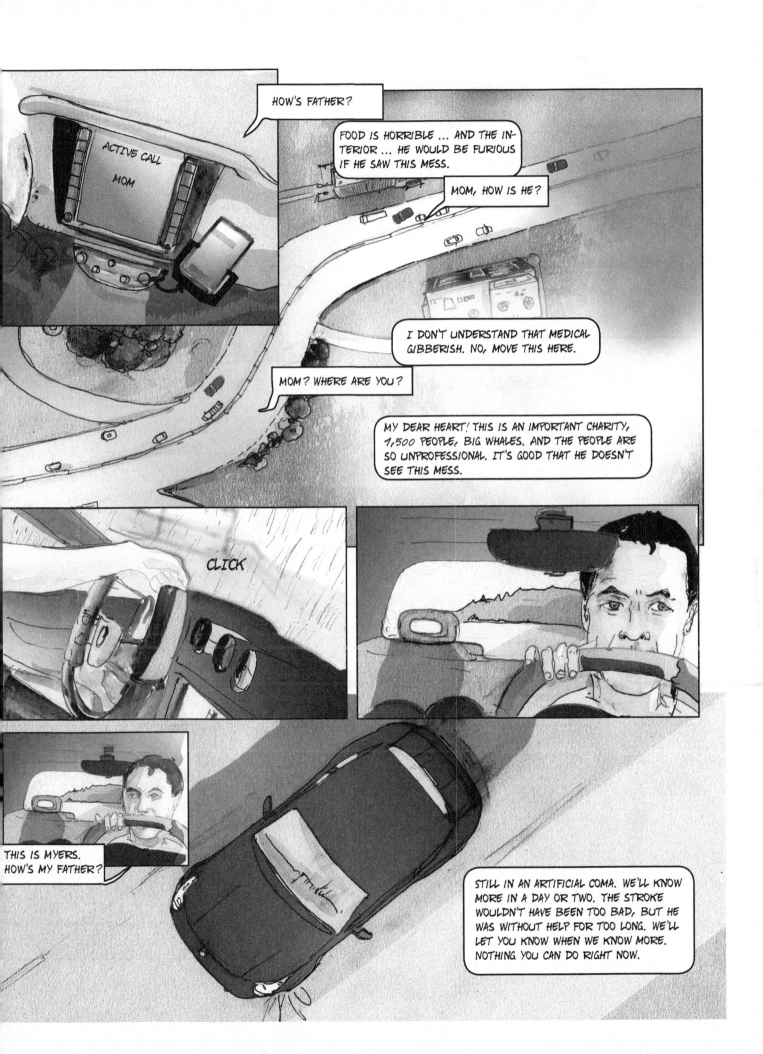

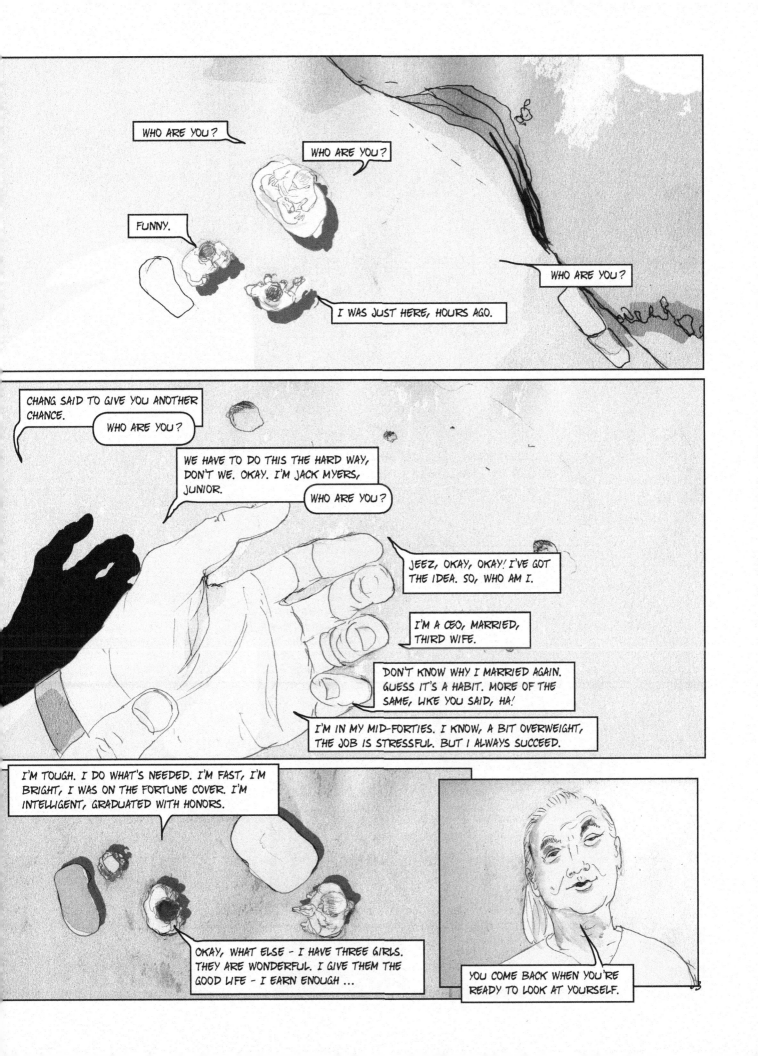

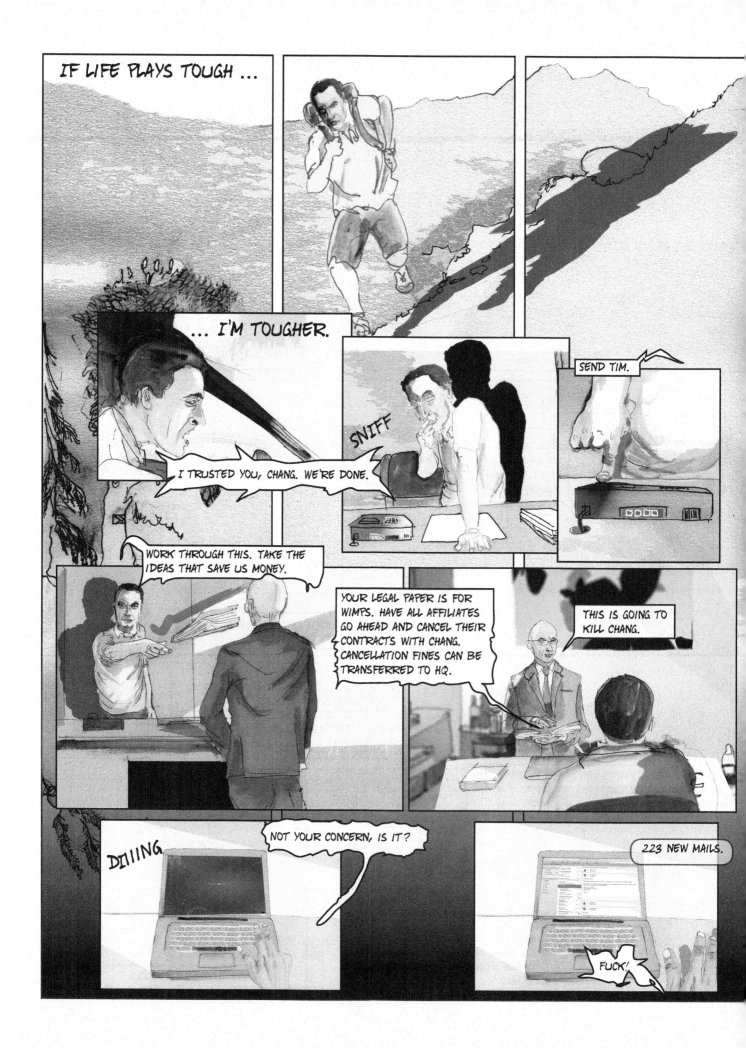

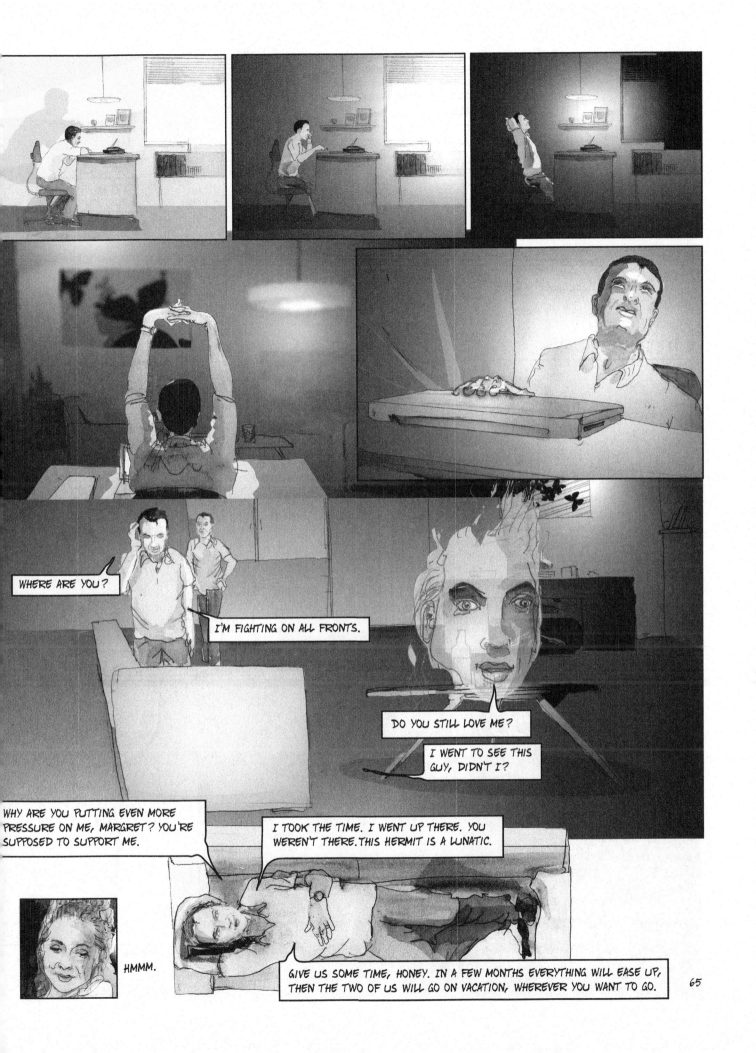

65

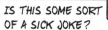

LATER THAT DAY ...

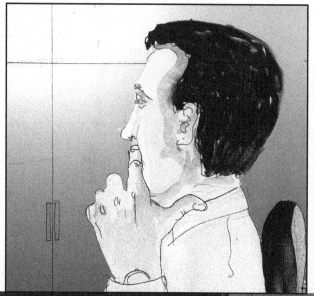

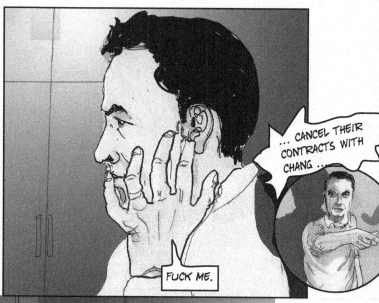

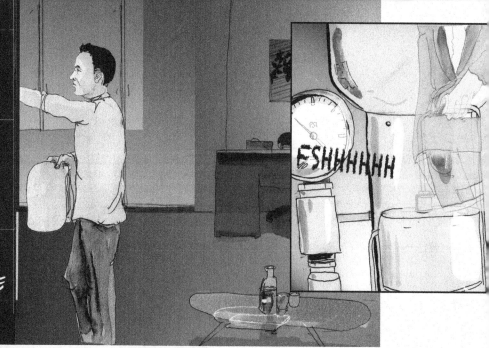

I WAS SO BUSY TRYING TO STAY IN CONTROL, TO STAY AHEAD OF THE GAME.

IT NEVER OCCURRED TO ME THAT I MIGHT BE PART OF THE PROBLEM.

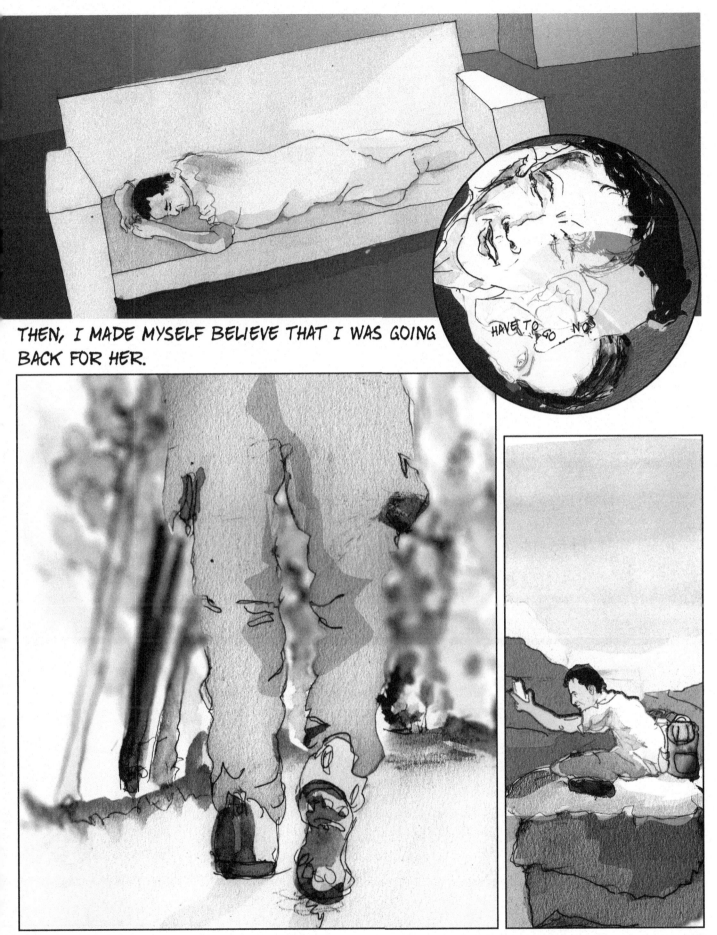

THEN, I MADE MYSELF BELIEVE THAT I WAS GOING BACK FOR HER.

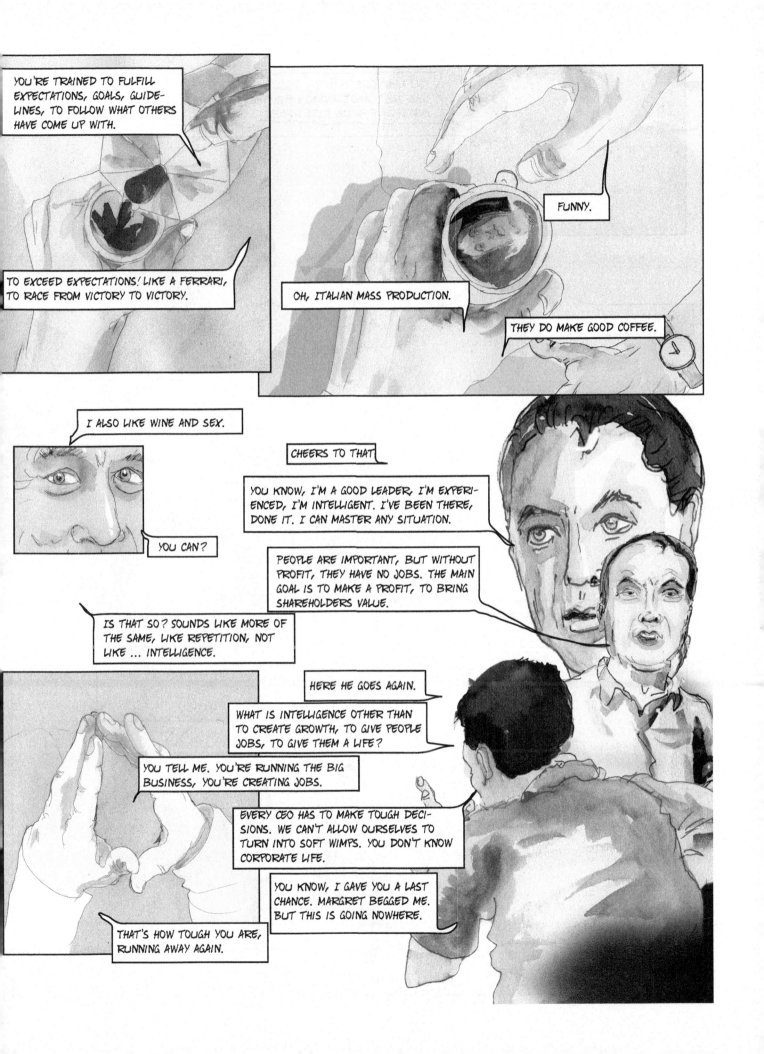

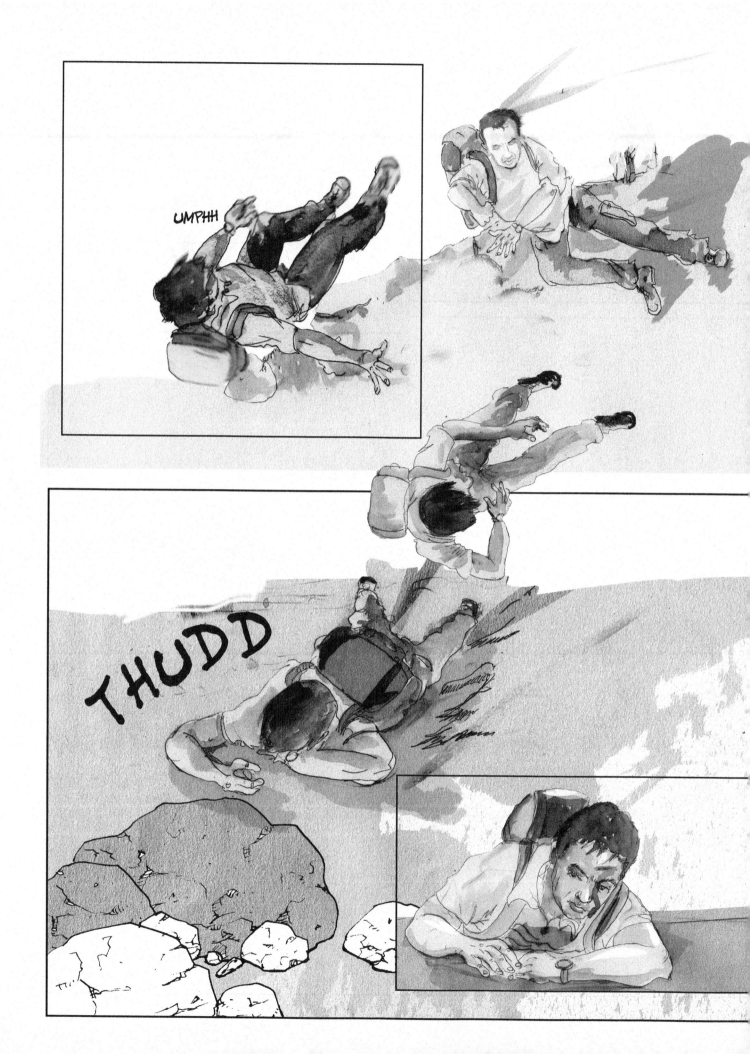

THIS TIME, I KNEW WHY I WENT BACK — I DID IT FOR MYSELF.

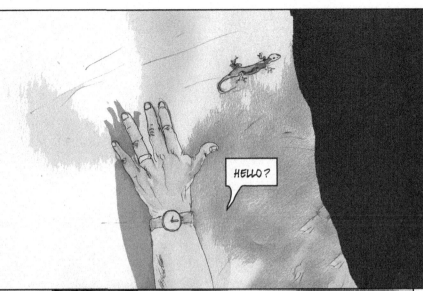

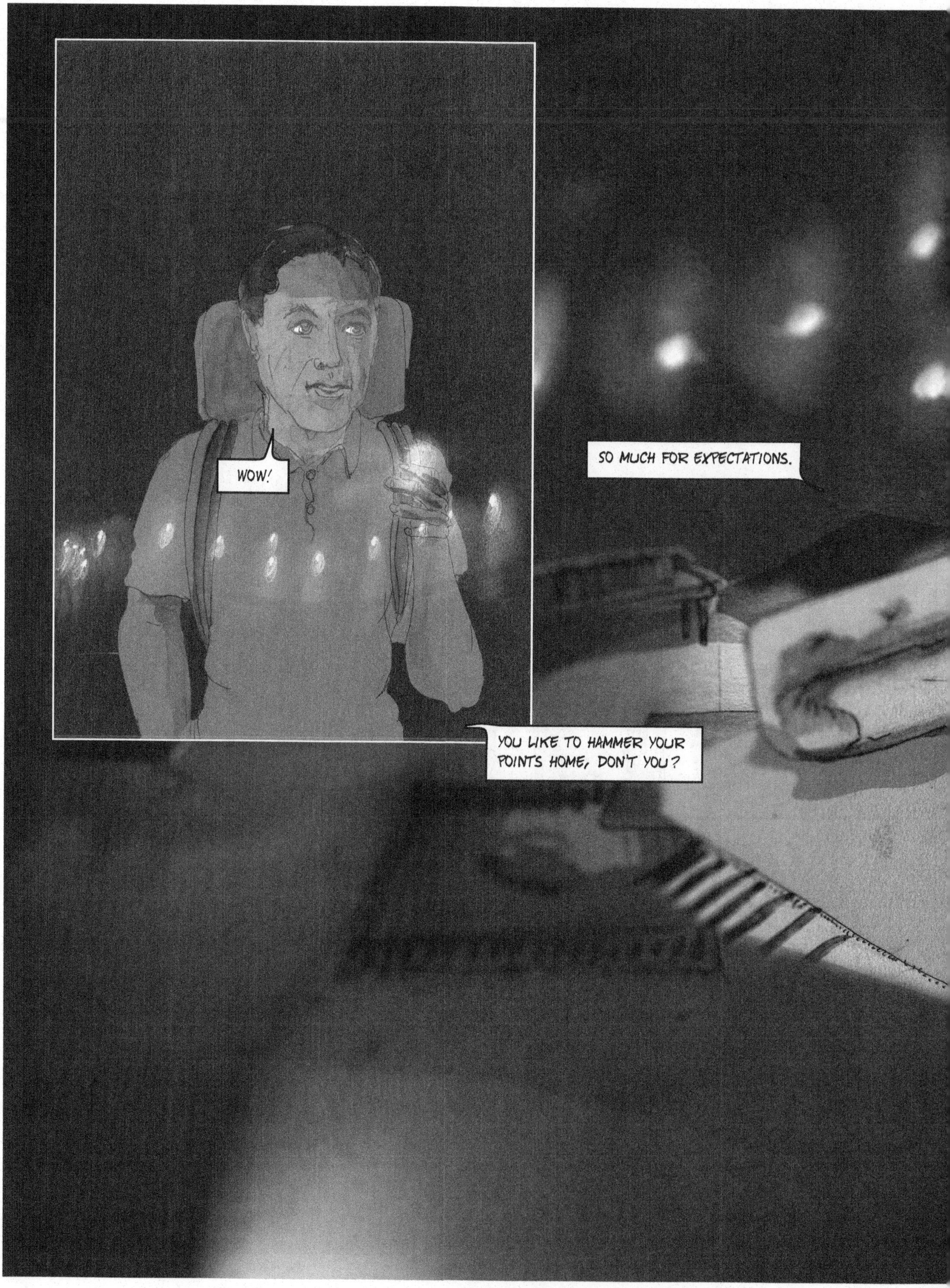
WOW!
SO MUCH FOR EXPECTATIONS.
YOU LIKE TO HAMMER YOUR POINTS HOME, DON'T YOU?

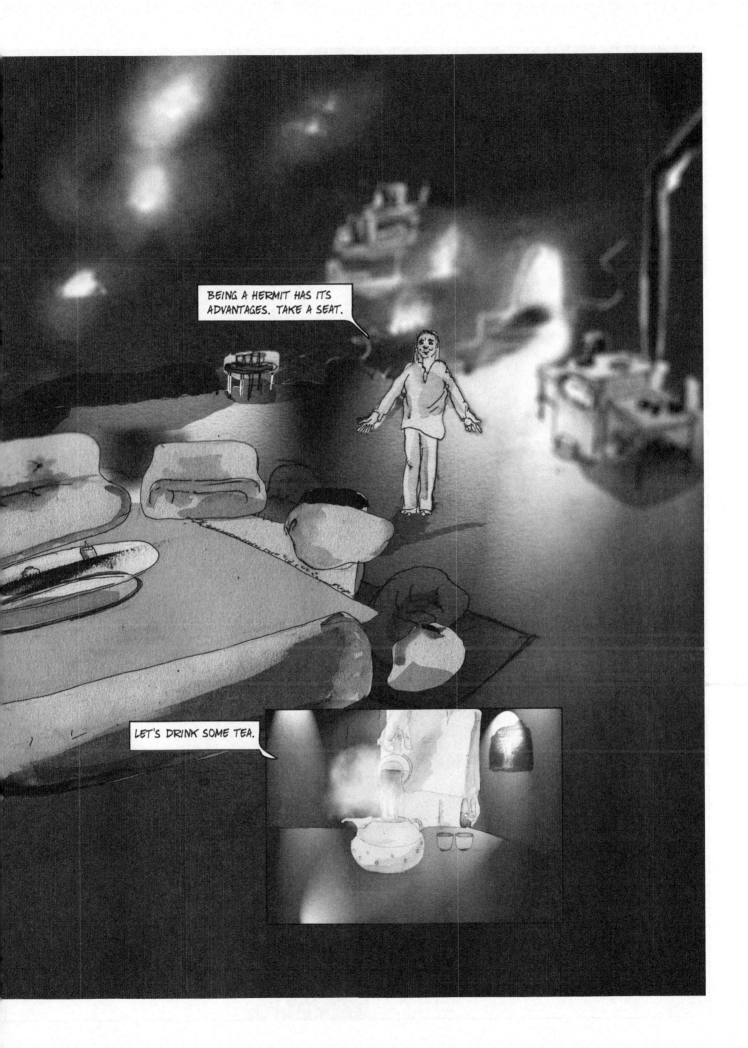

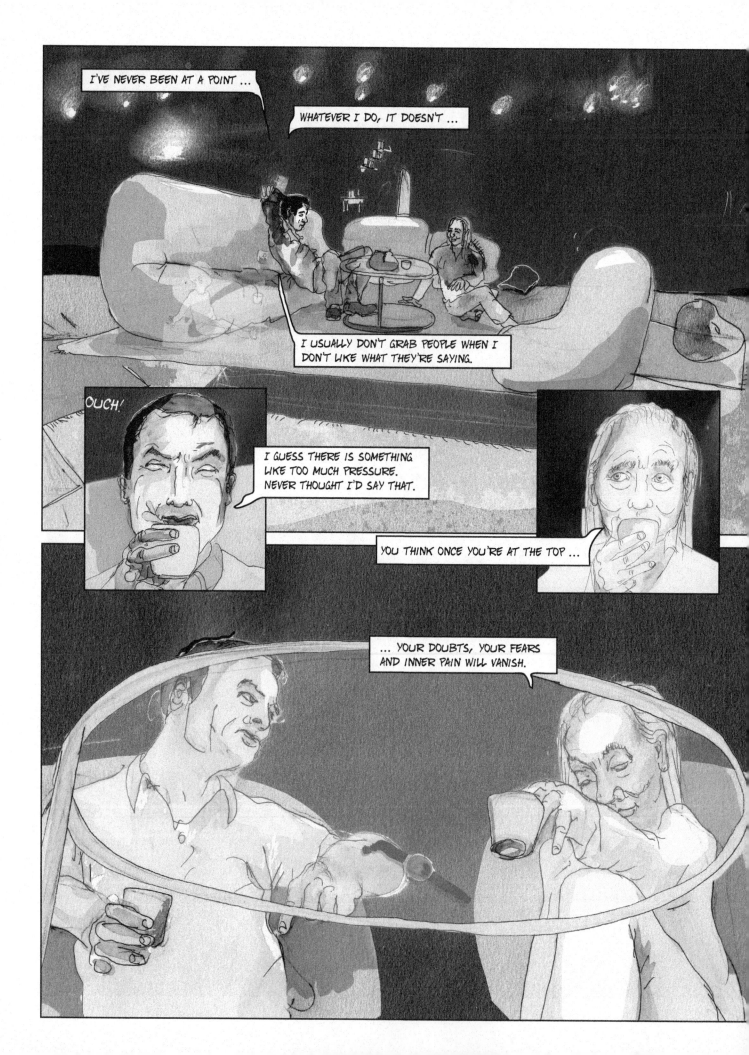

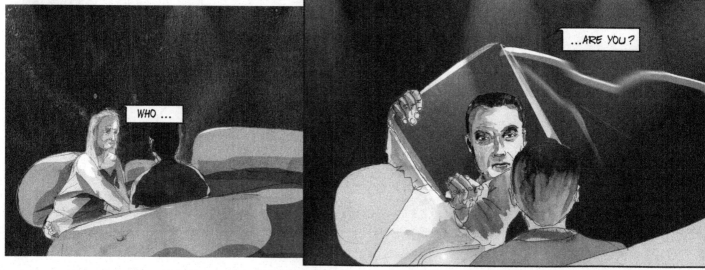

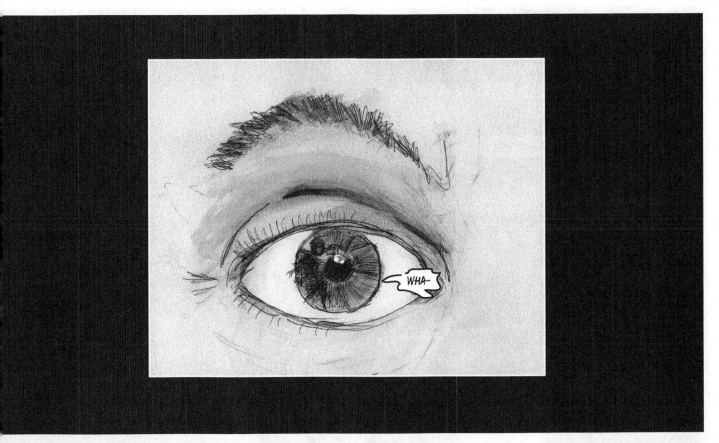

THEN, I WAS NOT READY TO REALIZE WHAT I'D SEEN. I WAS TOO FOCUSED ON MY GOALS, RELIED TO MUCH ON WHAT HAD WORKED UP TO NOW, ON THE STRATEGIES THAT HAD BROUGHT ME TO WHERE I WAS.

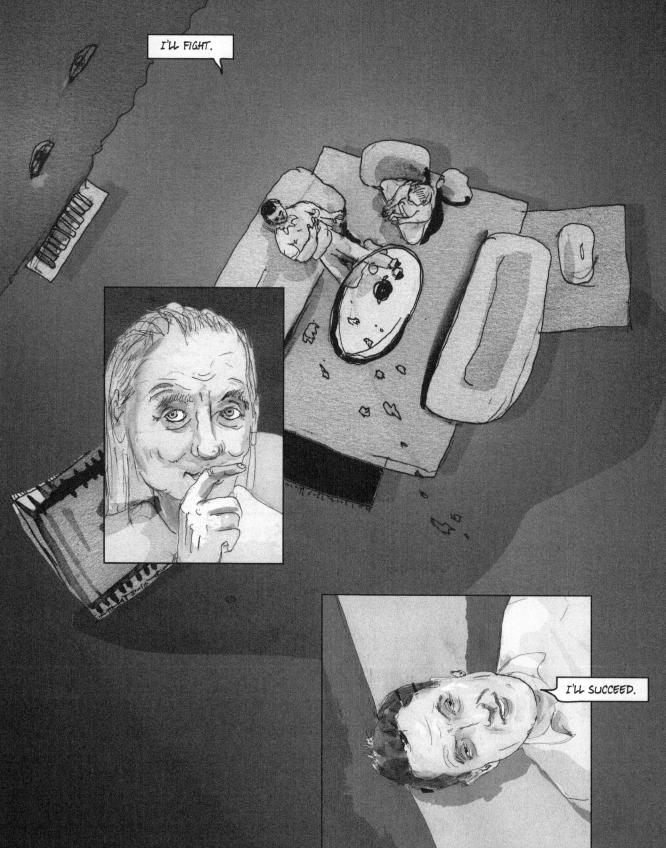

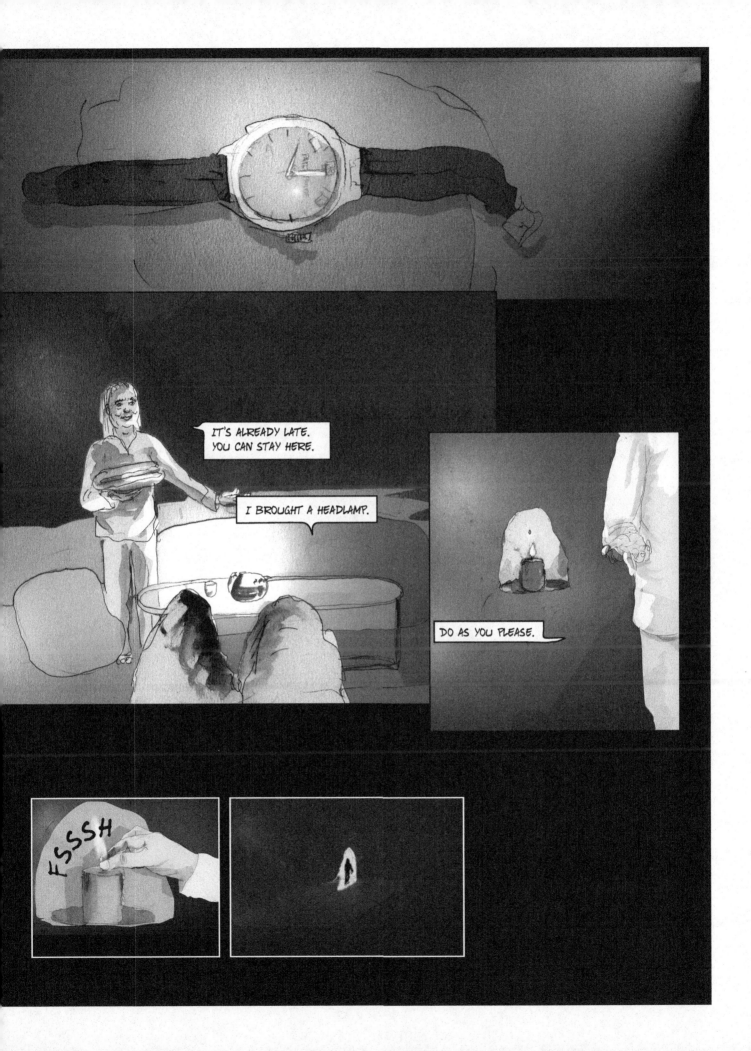

NO SIGNAL..
....
....
.............: .....

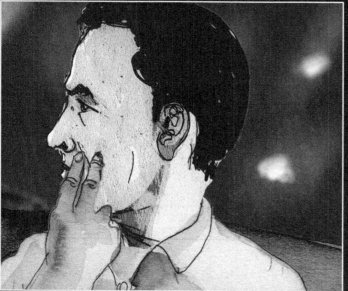

H-HM.

AT LEAST I WAS READY TO HIT THE BRAKES ...

... TO STOP ...

... TO SLOW DOWN FROM MY USUAL SPEE

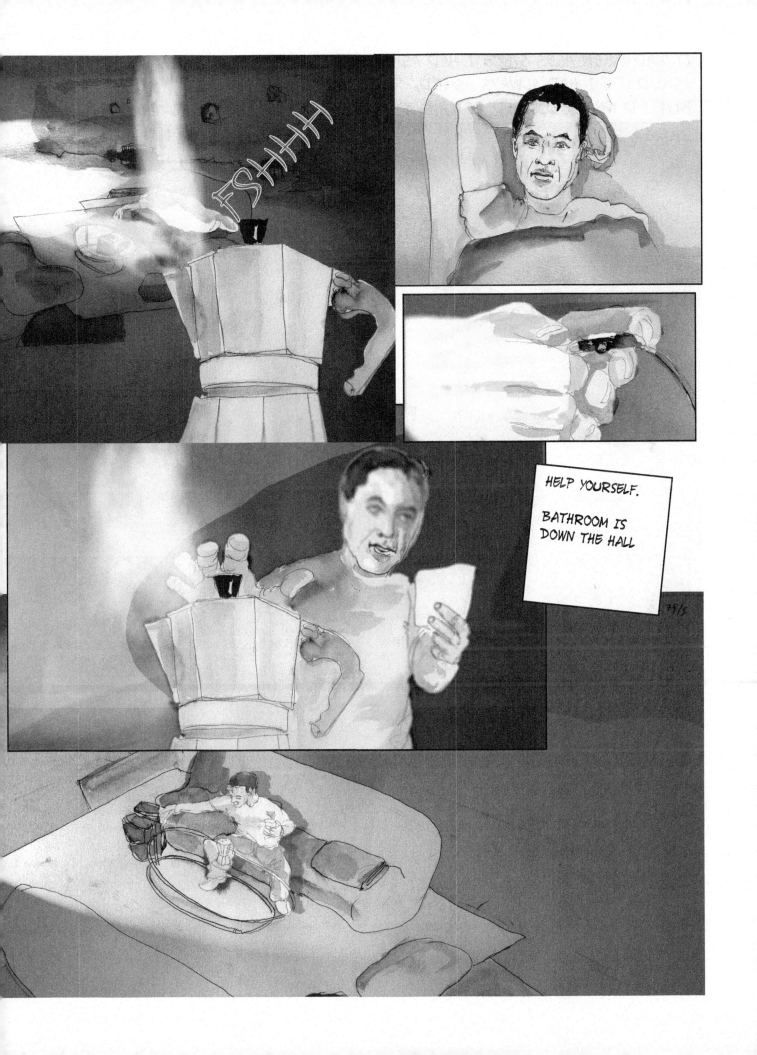

IT HAD BEEN AGES SINCE I HAD ASKED MYSELF THIS QUESTION. OR HAD I EVER ASKED IT? I HAD ALWAYS ASKED, "WHAT DO I WANT?"
BUT I'D NEVER LOOKED AT THIS "I." I HAD NEVER ASKED WHO THIS "I" WAS.

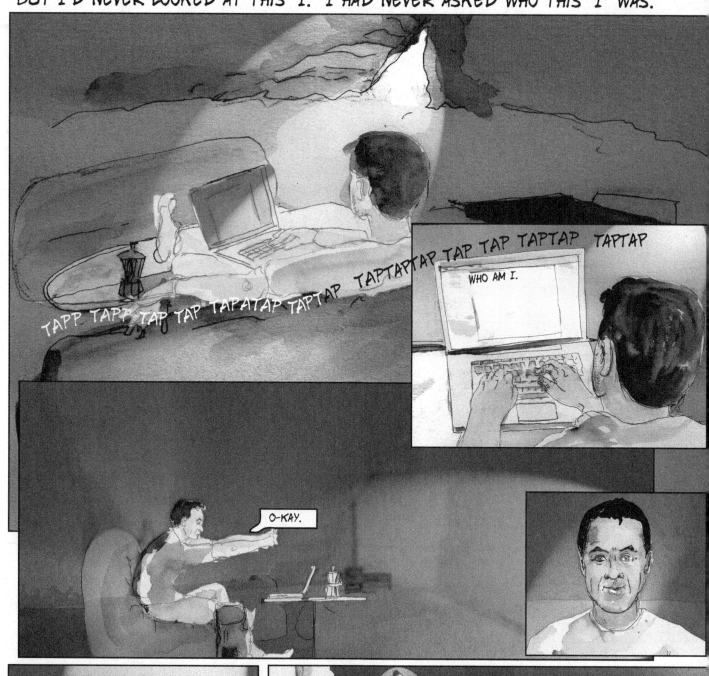

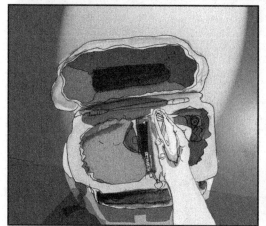

SOMETHING HAPPENED THEN ...

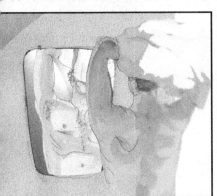  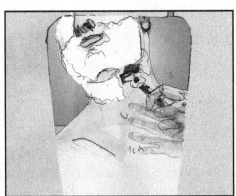

... AND AGAIN I DIDN'T REALIZE WHAT WAS HAPPENING.

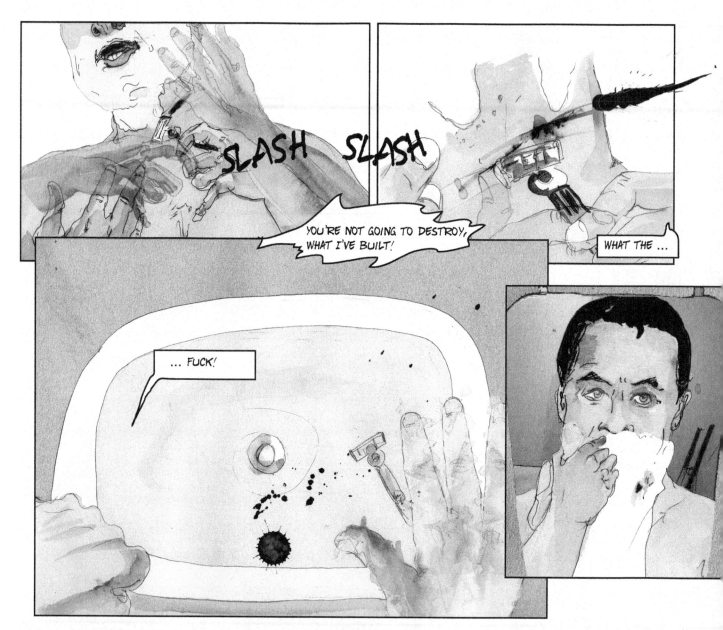

I SHOULD HAVE BEEN SCARED. I WASN'T. I HAD FORGOTTEN HOW TO BE SCARED.

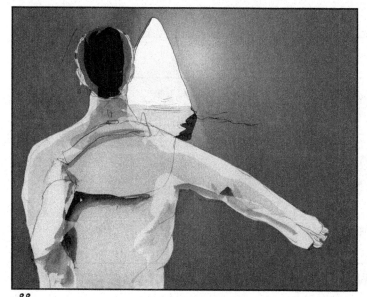

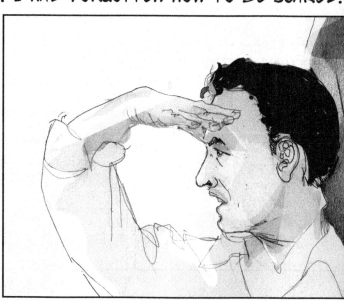

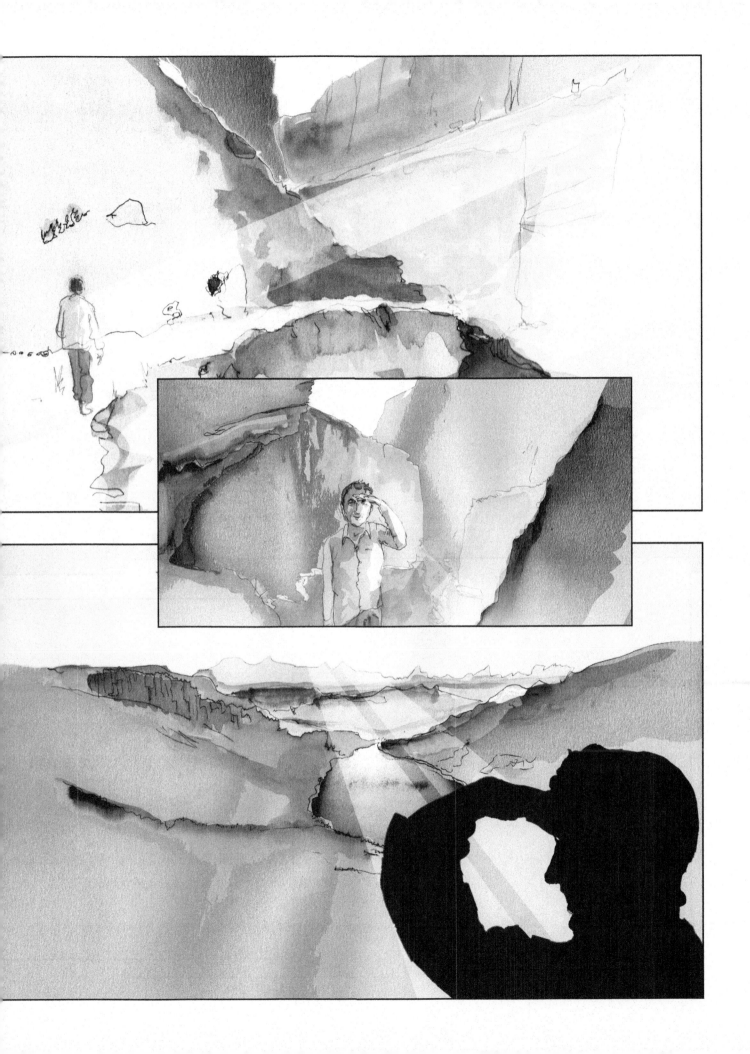

THERE WAS NO NEED FOR WORDS ...

... BUT AFTER A WHILE I NOTICED MYSELF SINGING, VERY SOFTLY.

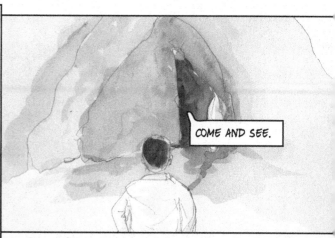

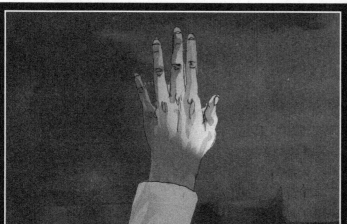

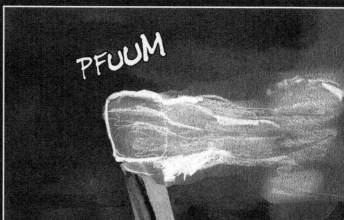

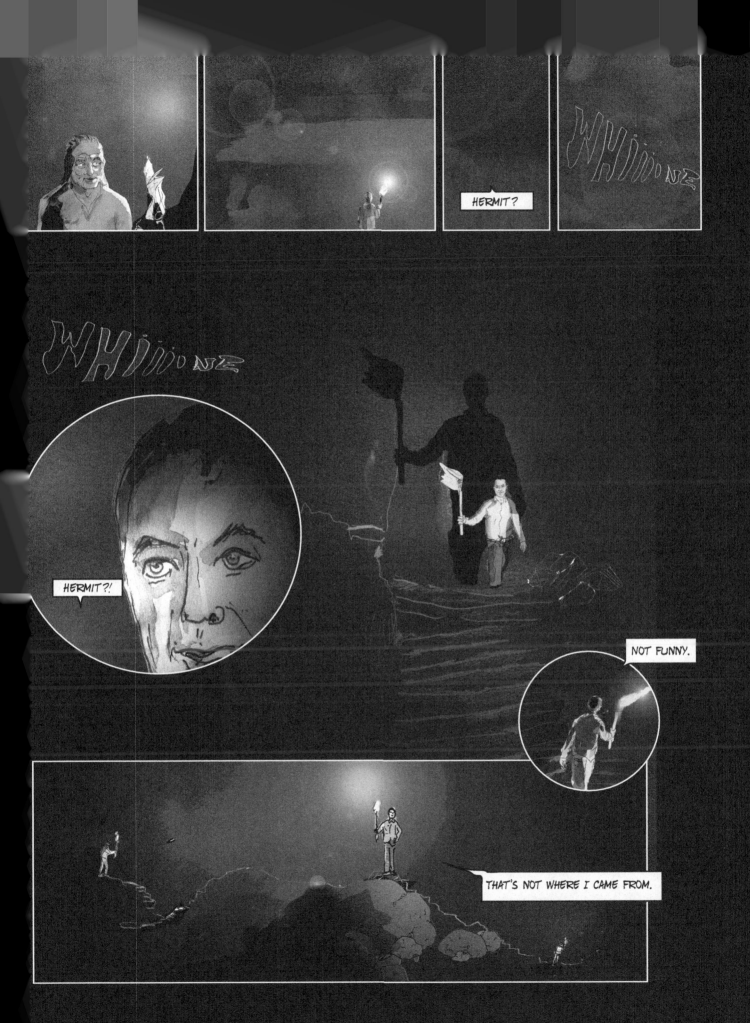

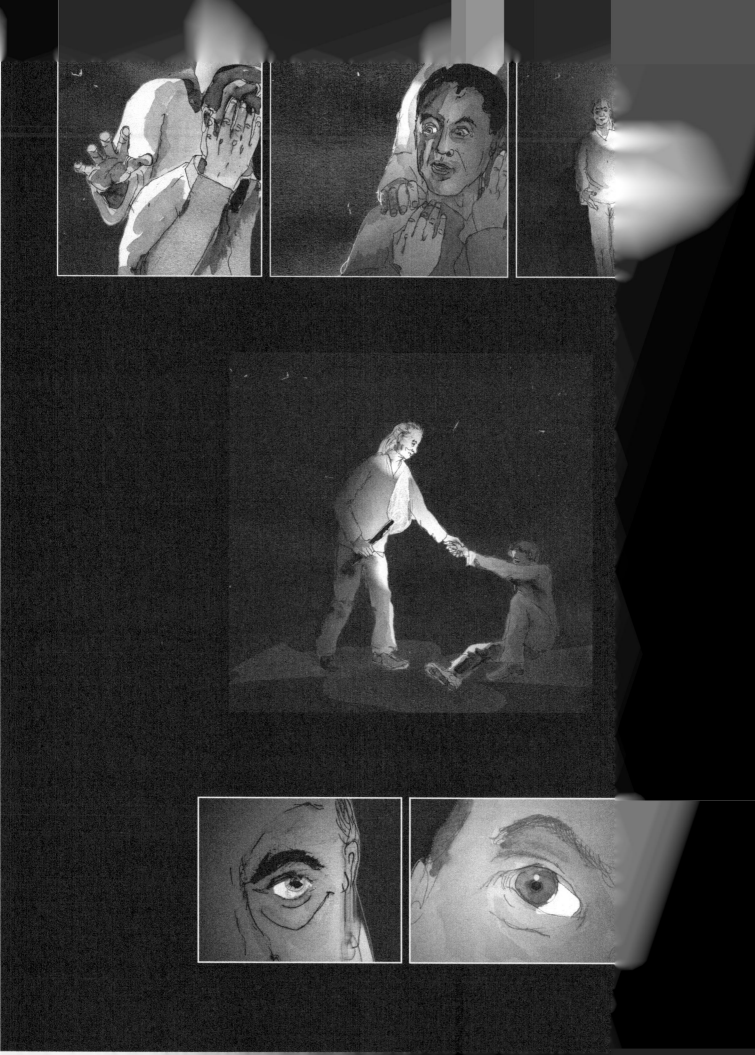

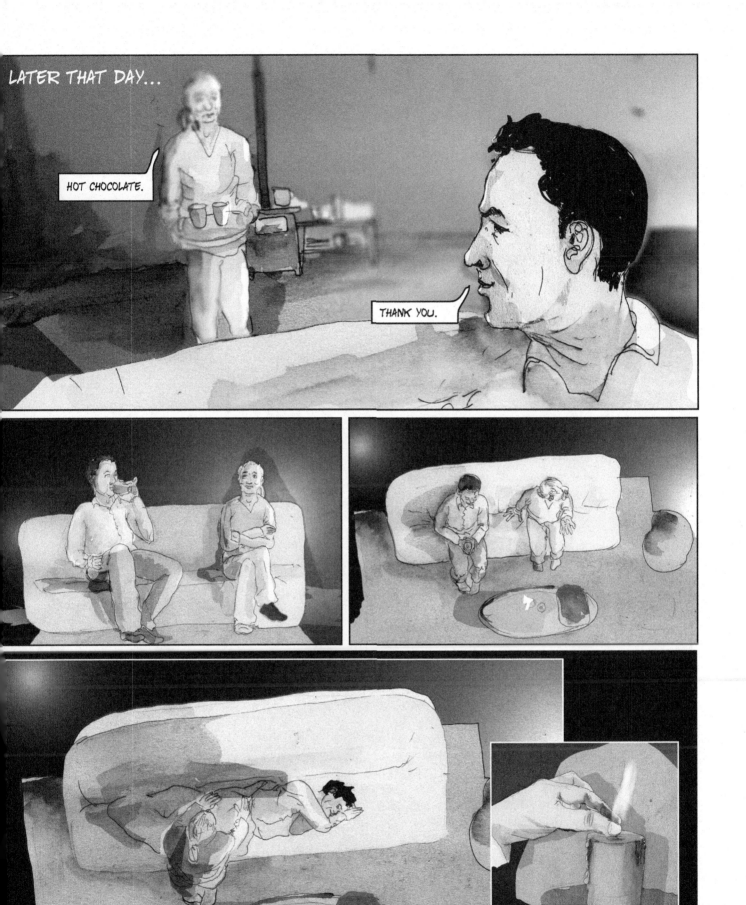

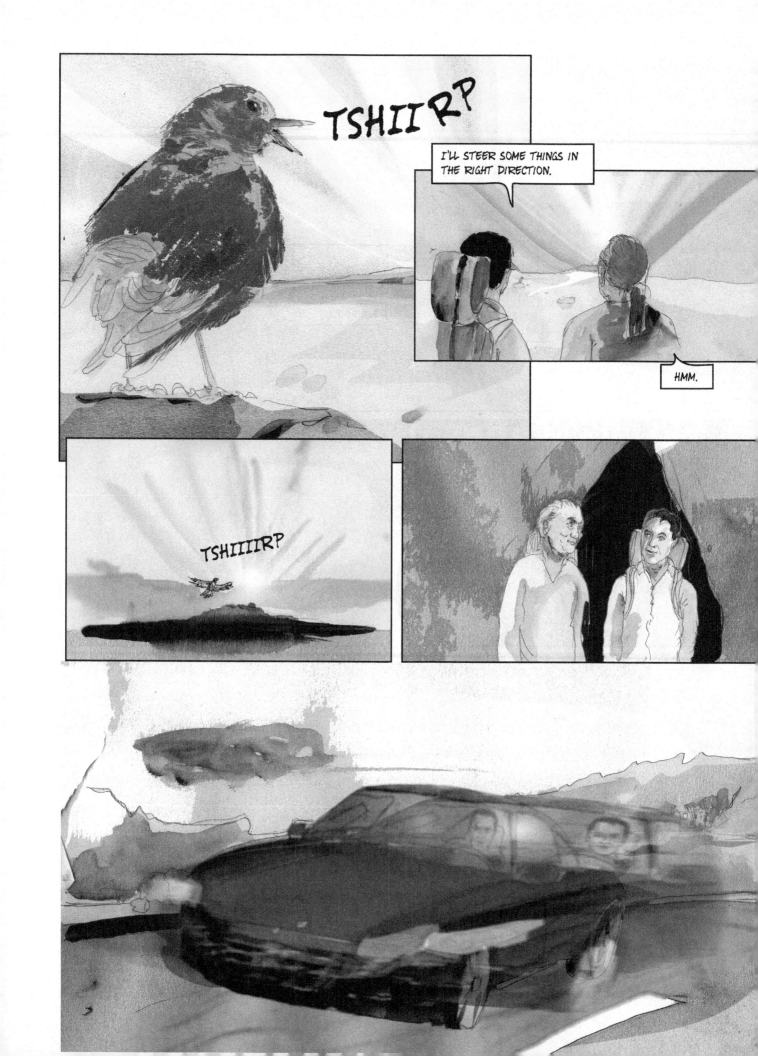

YOU GOTTA BE KIDDING!

TIM AND CHANG HAVE OCCUPIED YOUR OFFICE.
THEY HAVE BEEN FIGHTING ALL DAY.

GUYS.

CHANG, I TOLD YOU,
WE'RE GOING TO ...

OH PLEASE, TIM, GET A ...

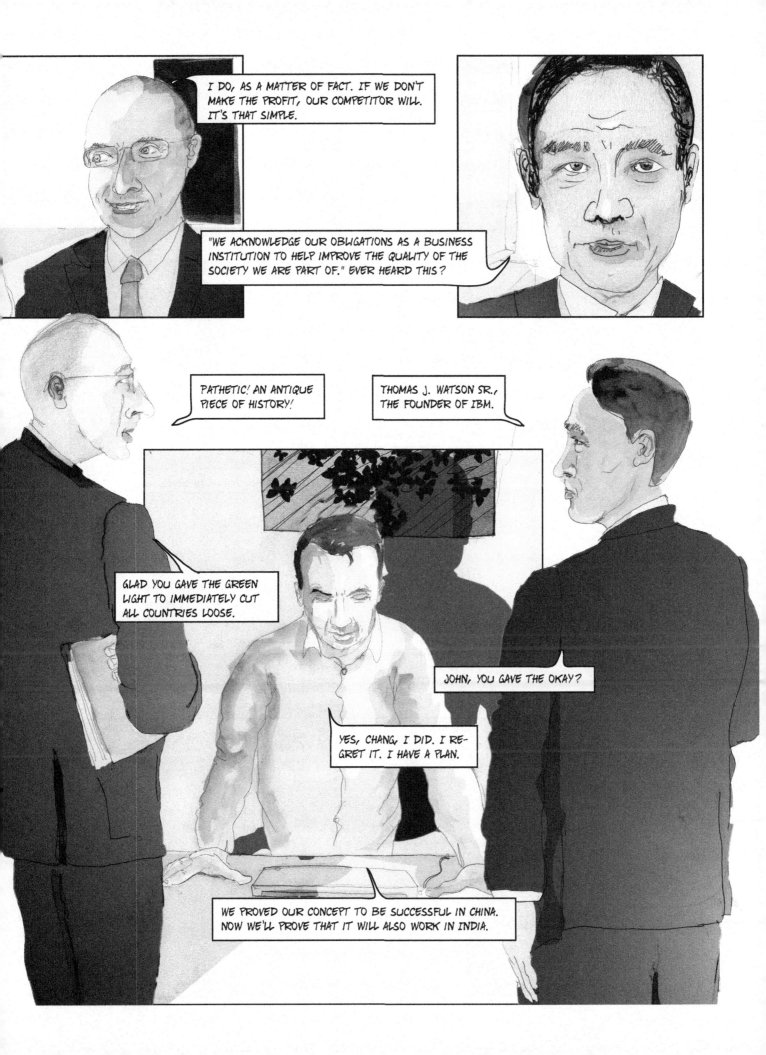

104

105

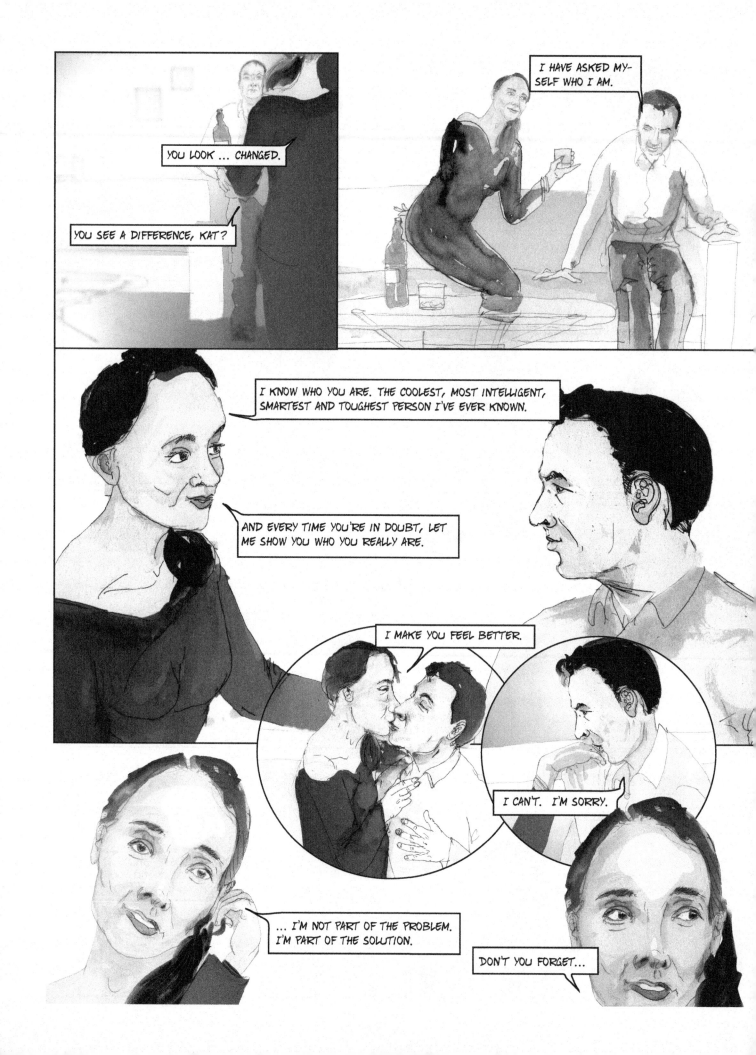

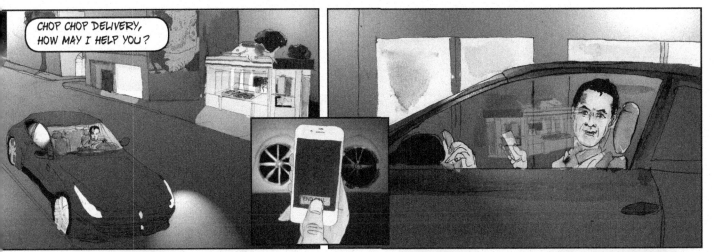

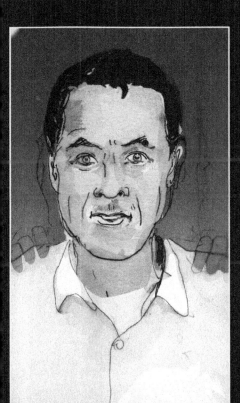

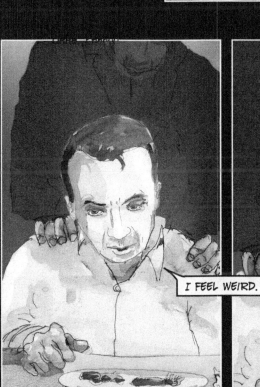

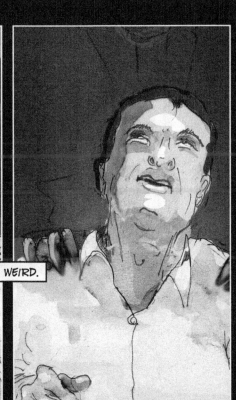

I CLEARLY REMEMBER THE MOMENT I REALIZED. SOMETHING WAS GOING ON.
THIS WAS THE SAME FEELING I HAD WHEN THE HERMIT SHOWED ME THE MIRROR.

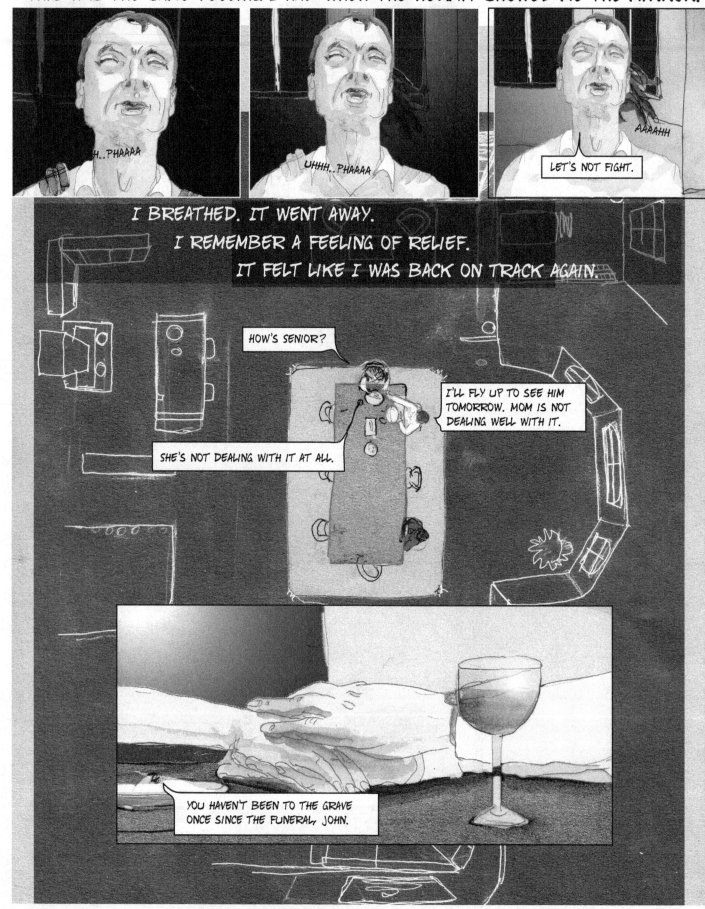

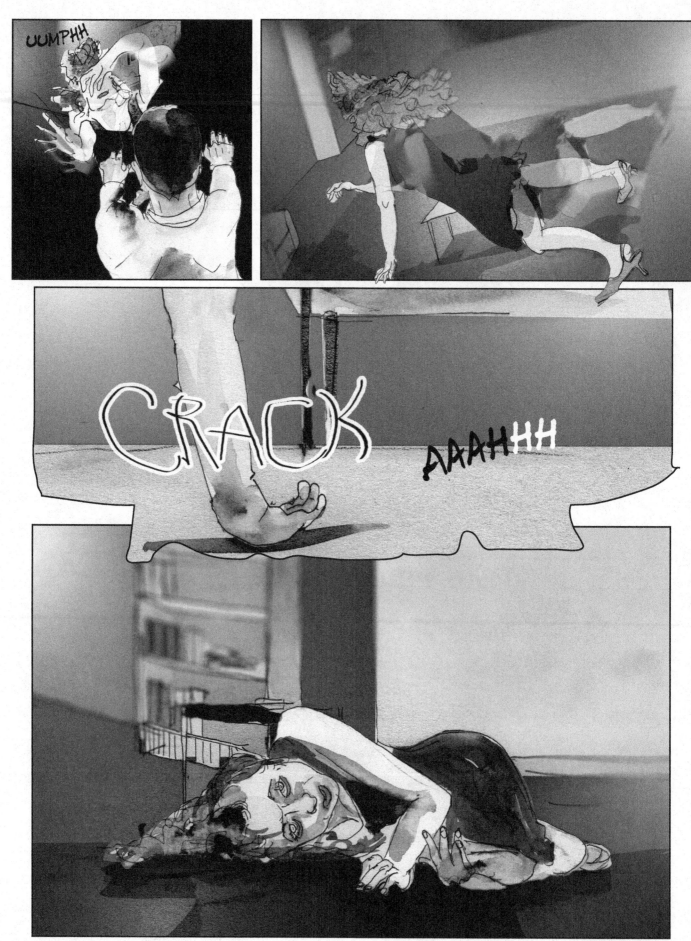

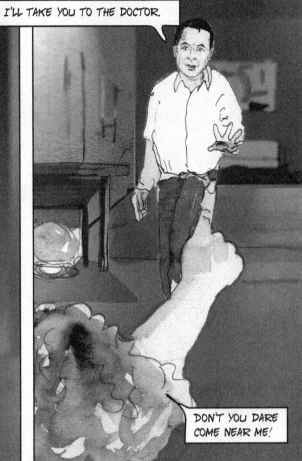

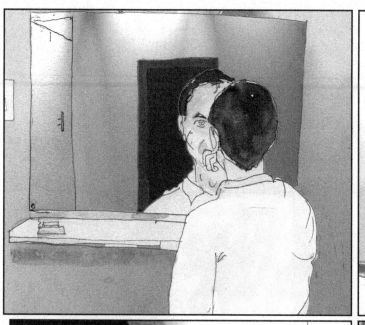
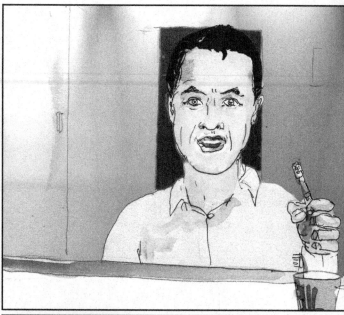
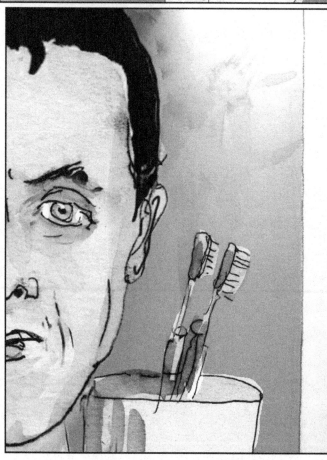
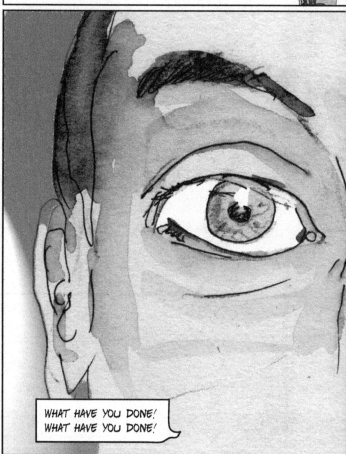

WHAT HAVE YOU DONE!
WHAT HAVE YOU DONE!

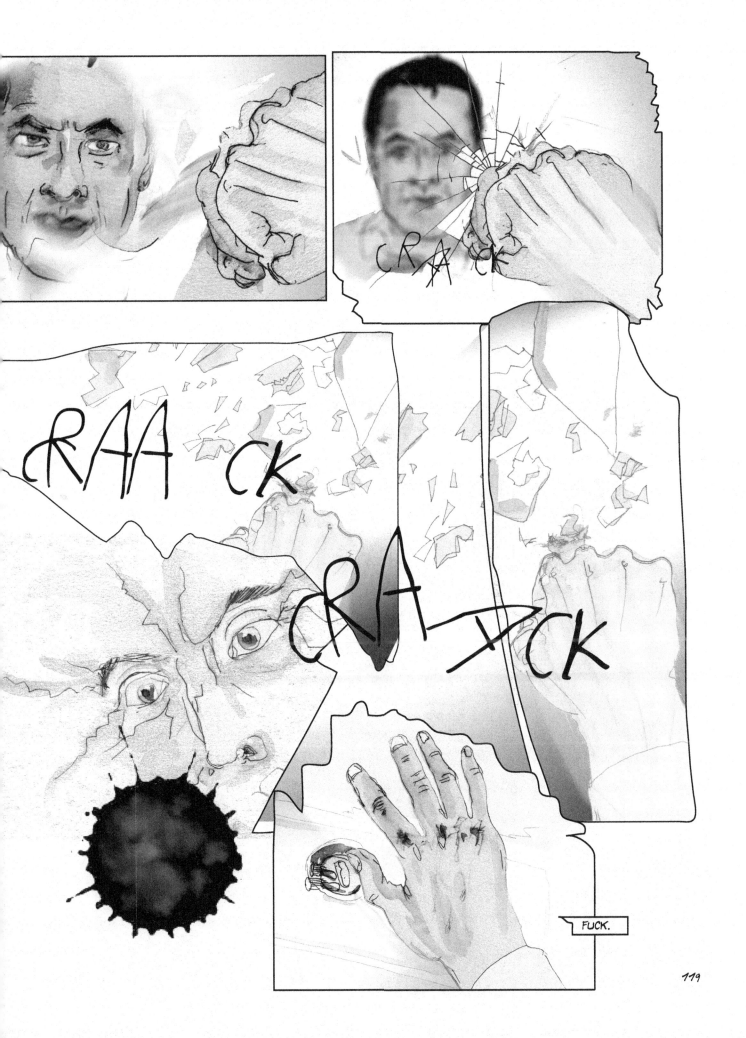

119

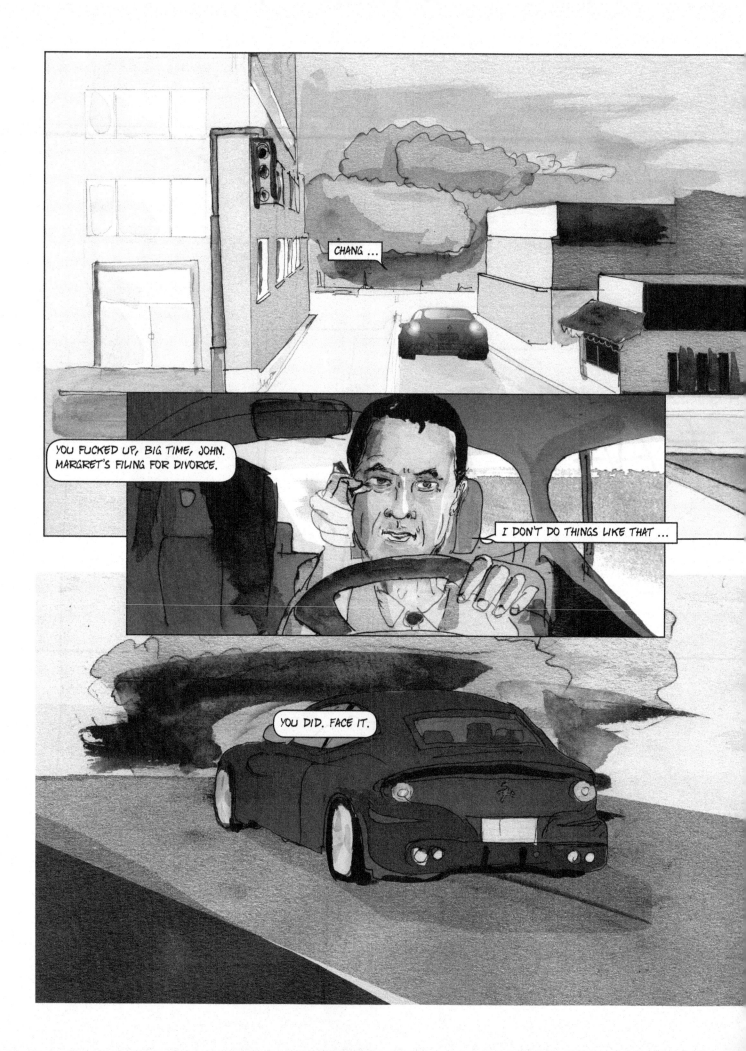

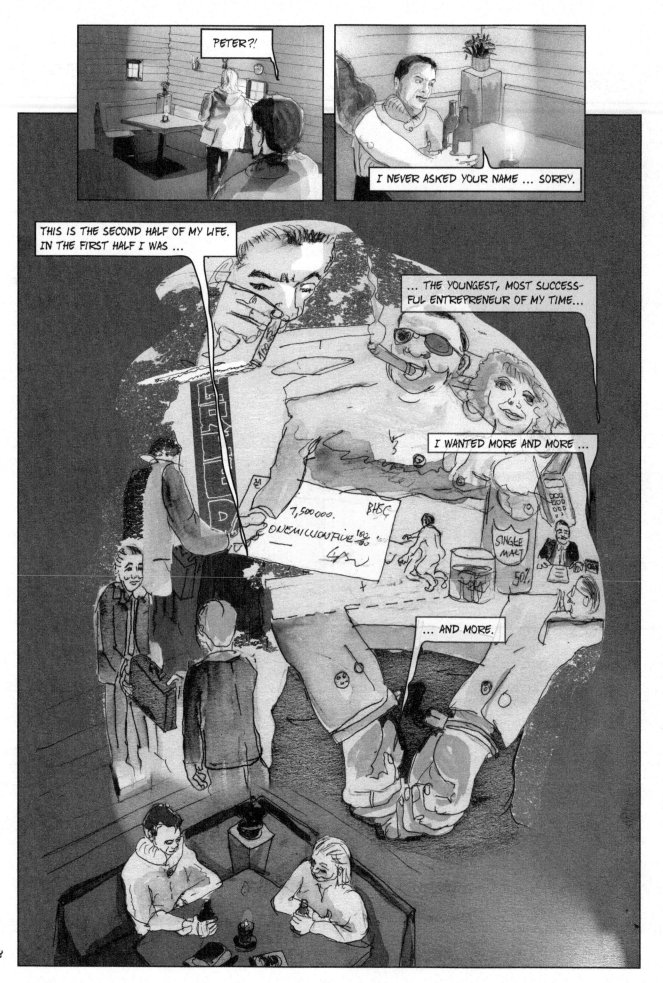

I HAVE TO FIND OUT, DON'T I?

VAAROooM

WHO AM I?

DAD, WE ...

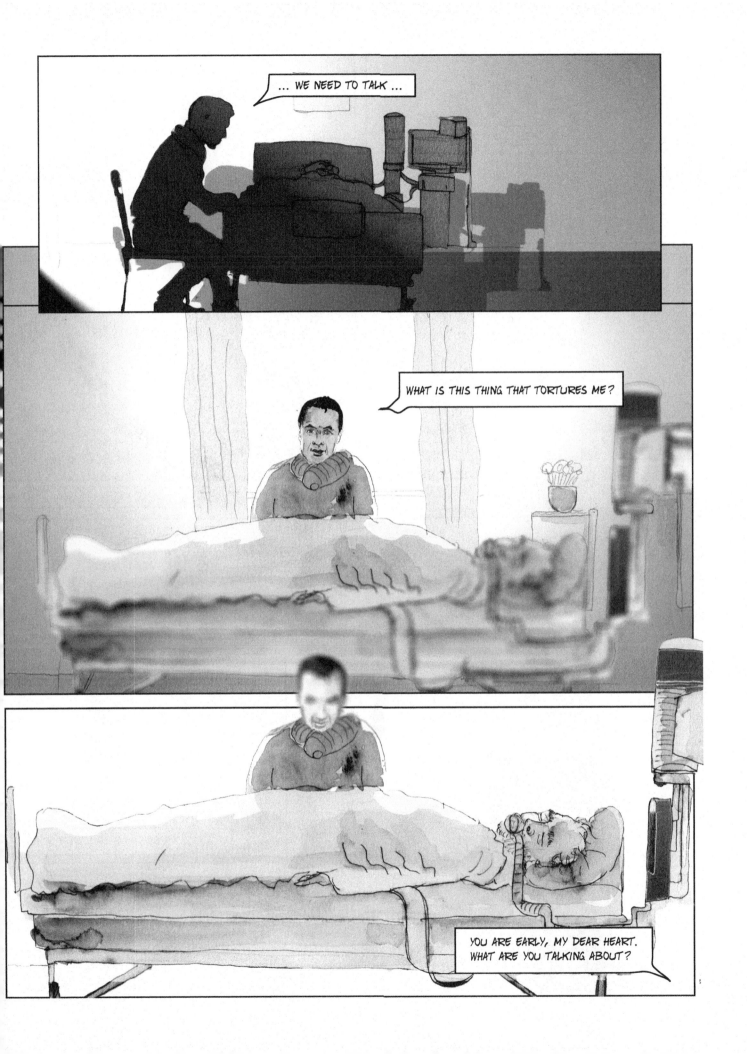

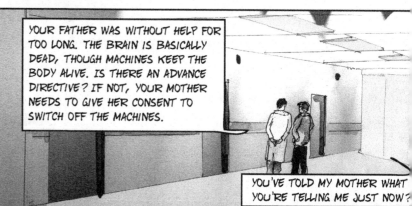

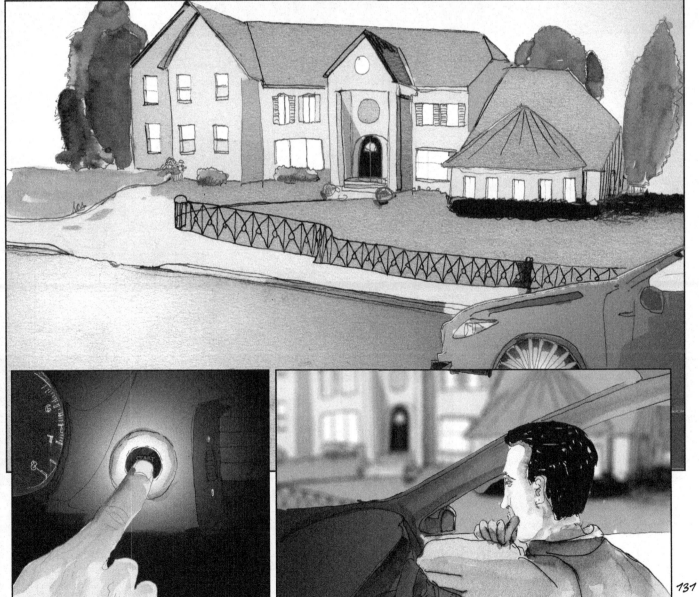

137

FOR THE FIRST TIME, MY INNER VOICE WAS NOT JUST A VOICE BUT ...

... AS IF ... SOMEONE REAL WAS TALKING DOWN TO ME.

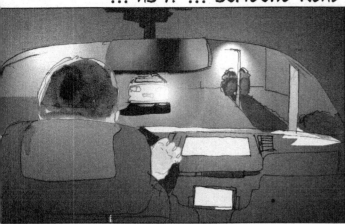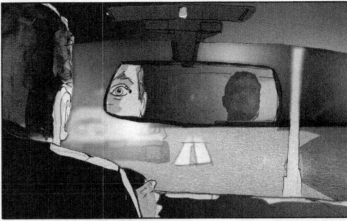

THE REALIZATION HIT ME HARD. THIS WAS IT.

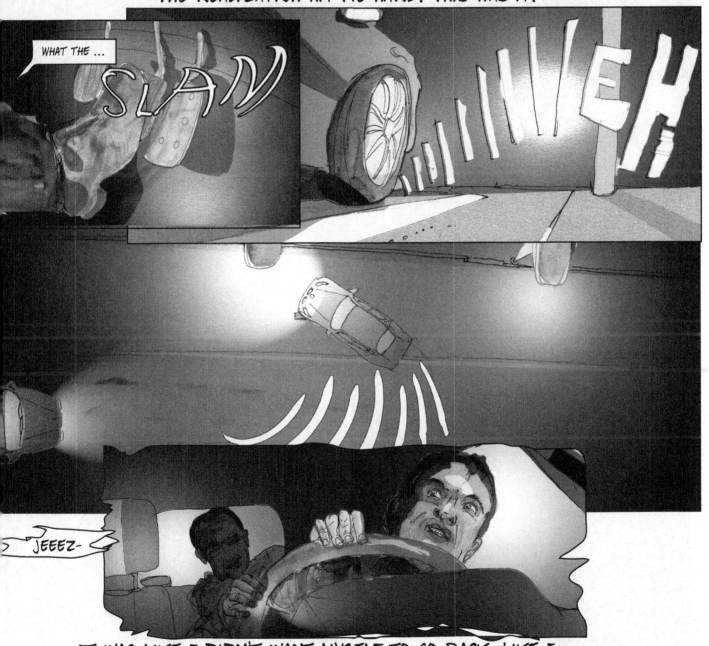

IT WAS LIKE I DIDN'T WANT MYSELF TO GO BACK. LIKE I
DIDN'T WANT MYSELF TO FIND WHATEVER WAS WAITING FOR ME.

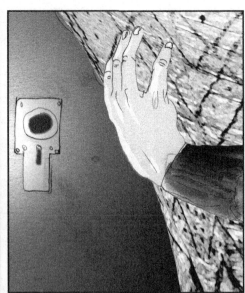

DAMN.

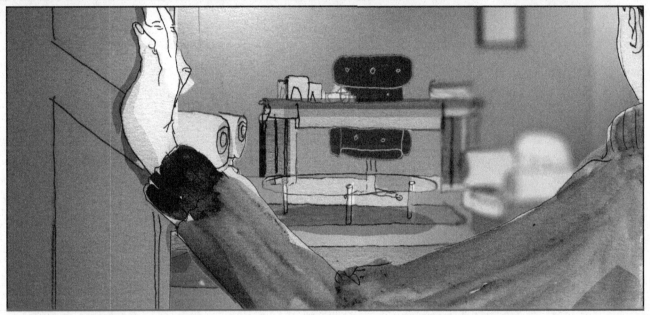

MY FATHER'S OFFICE. I CAN HARDLY REMEMBER THE FEW TIMES I WAS ALLOWED IN.

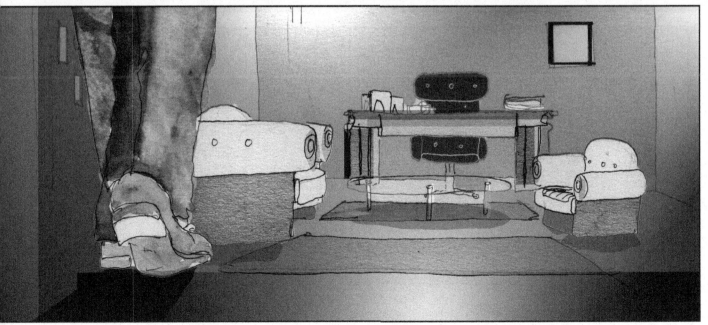

I HAD CERTAINLY NEVER BEEN BEHIND HIS DESK.

I COULDN'T HAVE TOLD YOU THEN, BUT NOW I KNOW IT WAS GUILT I FELT, SITTING IN HIS CHAIR.

AND THEN THE RECOGNITION SLOWLY SETTLING IN: HIS OFFICE AND MY OFFICE LOOKED VERY SIMILAR.

THERE WERE ALL MY CERTIFICATES — HANGING NEXT TO HIS DECORATIONS AND NEXT TO GRANDFATHER'S DECORATIONS FROM WORLD WAR II.

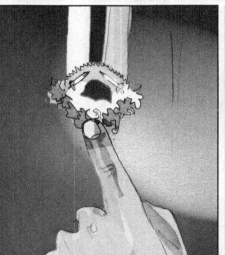

I WONDER...

I NEVER EVEN GOT CLOSE TO HIS AWARDS.

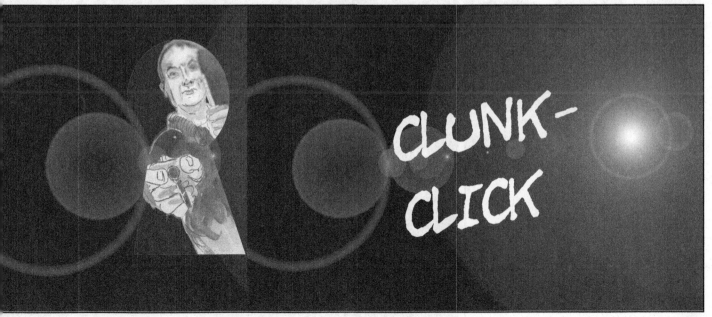

CLUNK-
CLICK

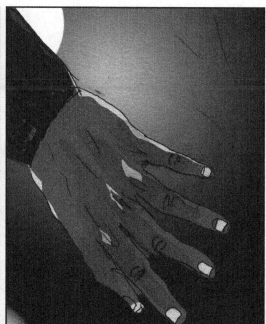

I NEEDED ...

... LIGHT.

CLICK

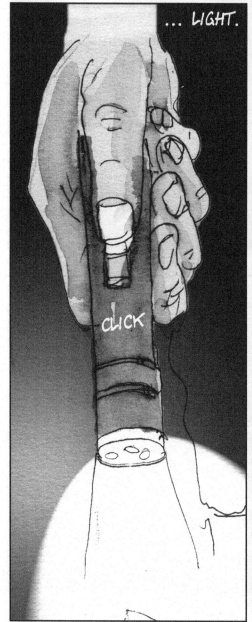

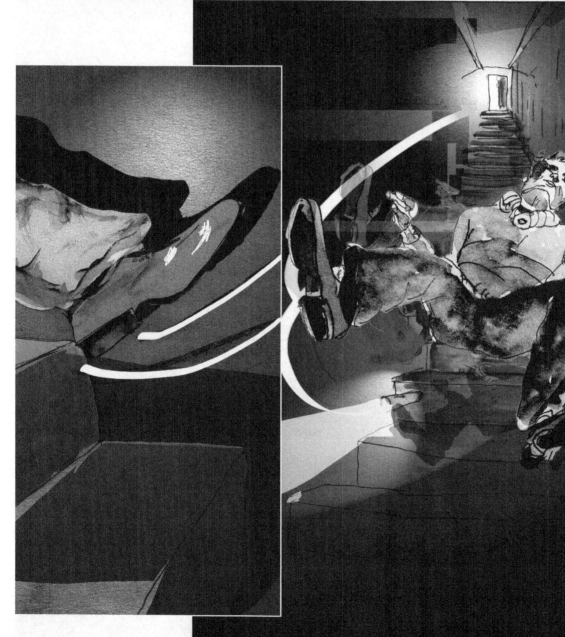

148

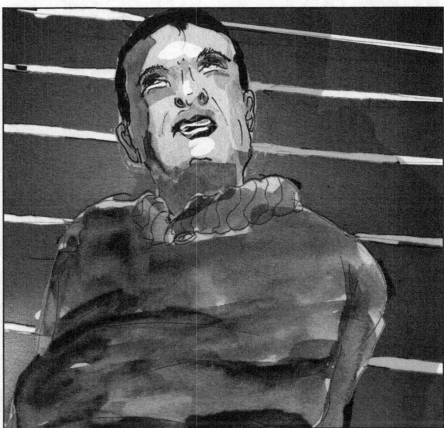

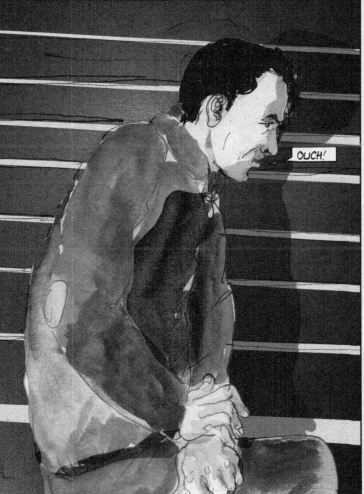

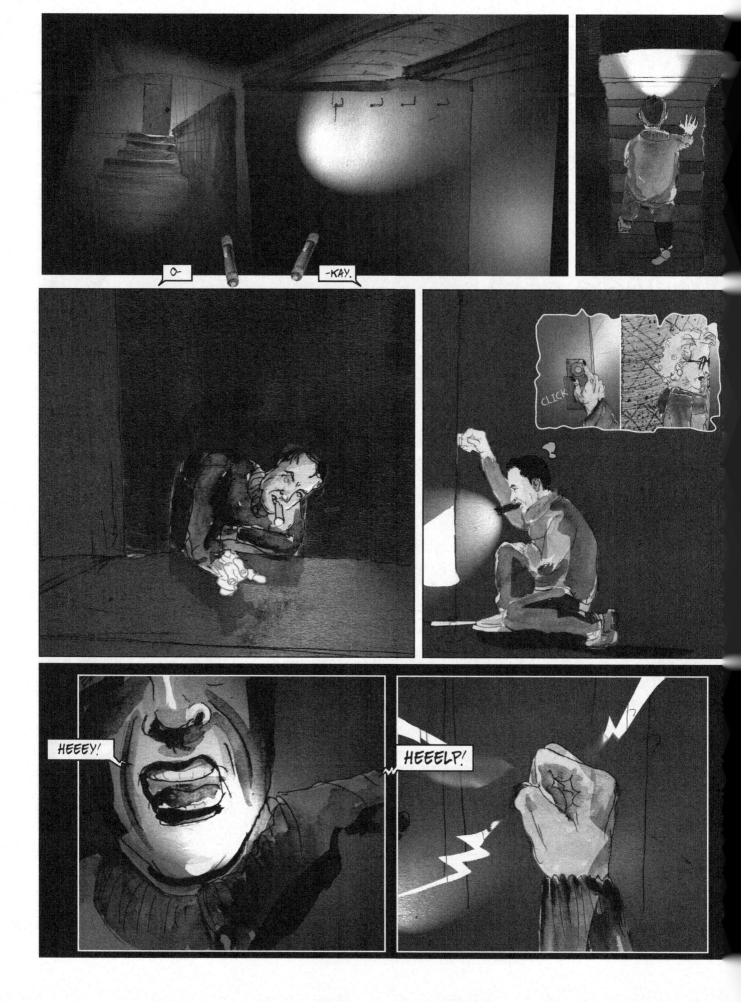

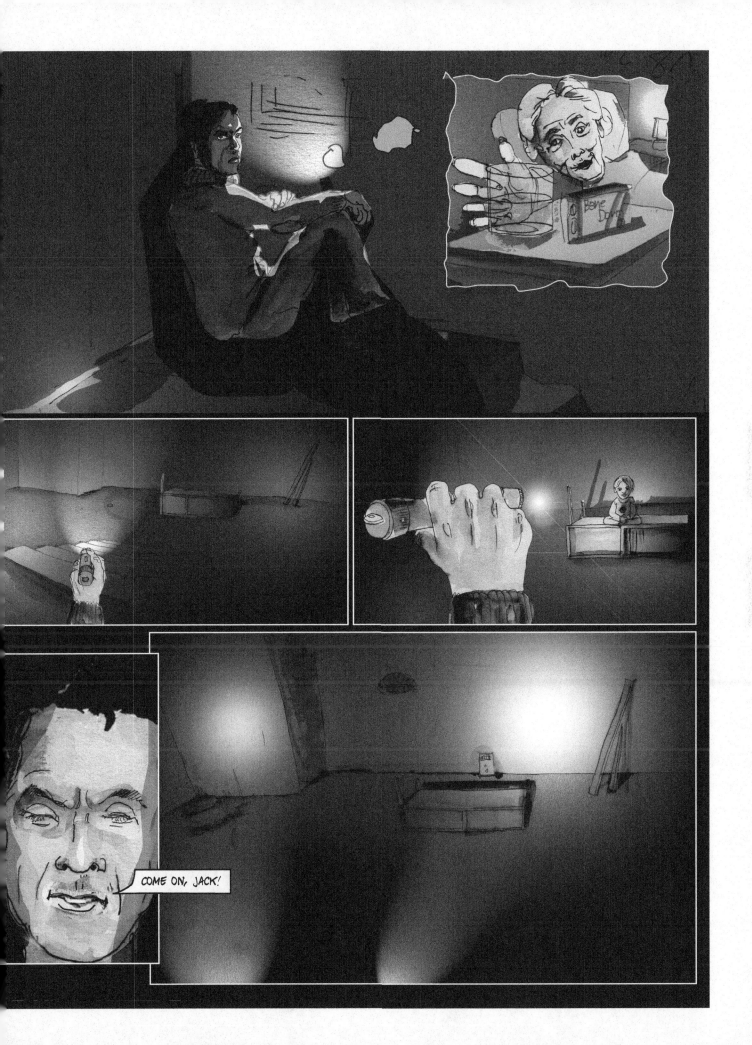

SORRY ABOUT THE LIGHT.

WELL.

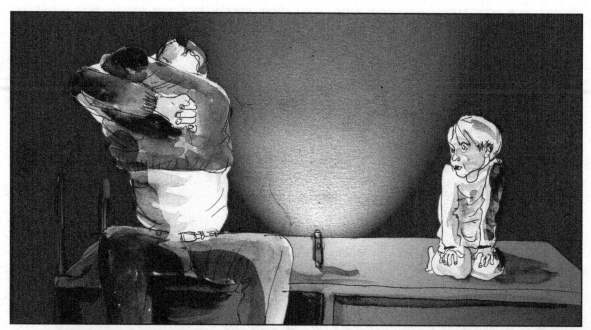

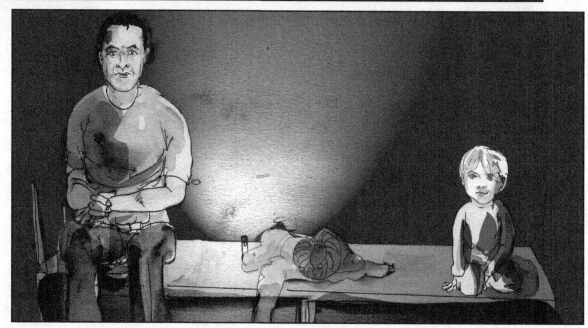

154

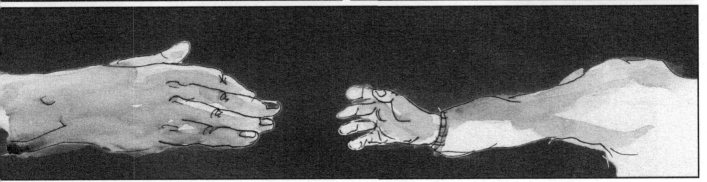

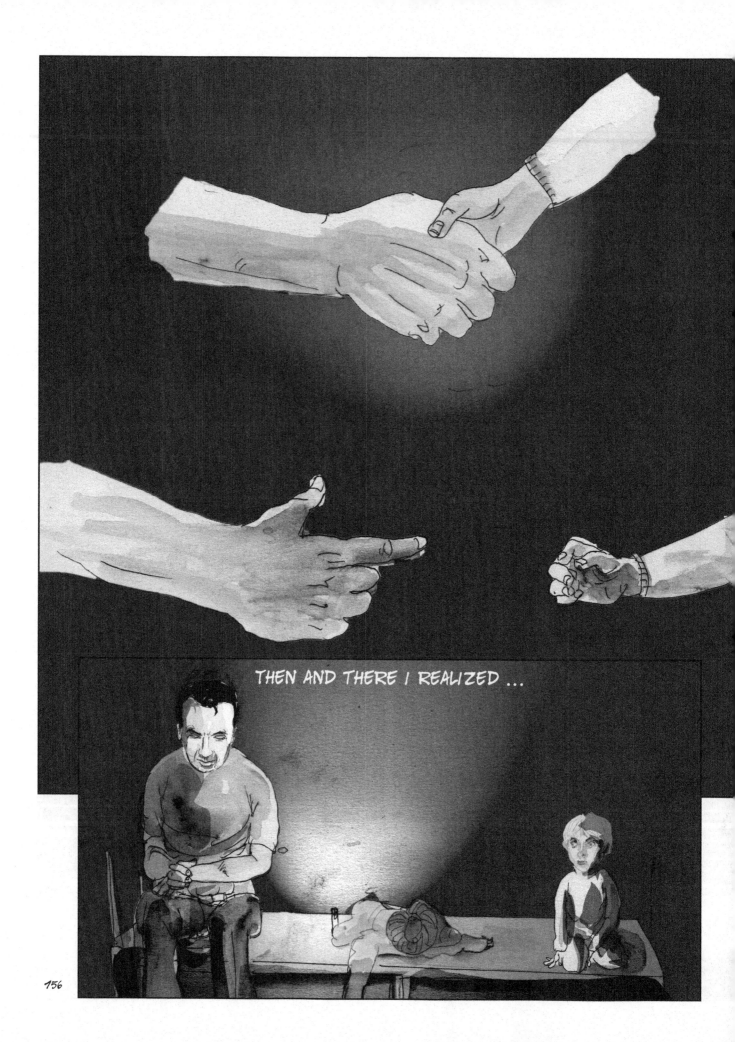

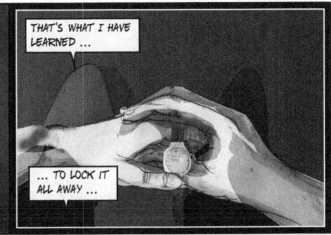

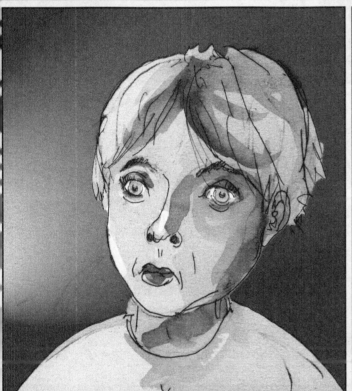

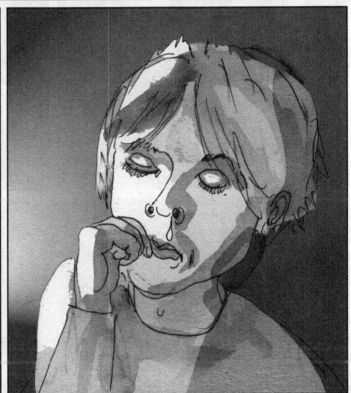

... I'M SO SORRY, I'M SO SORRY ...

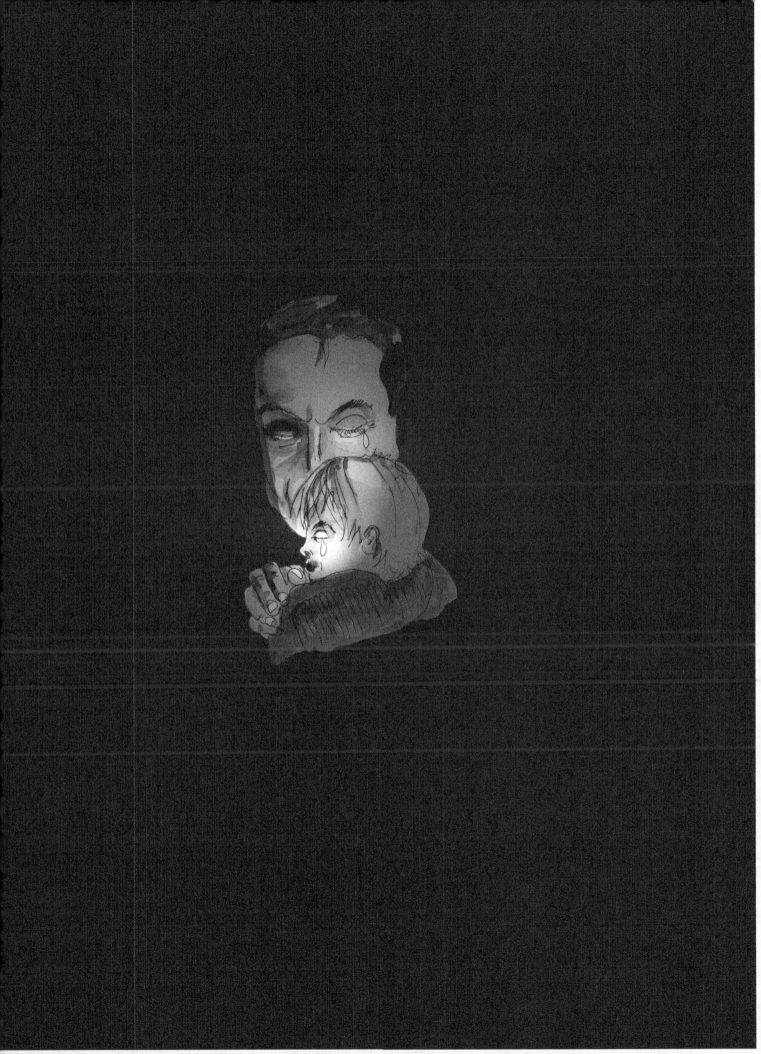

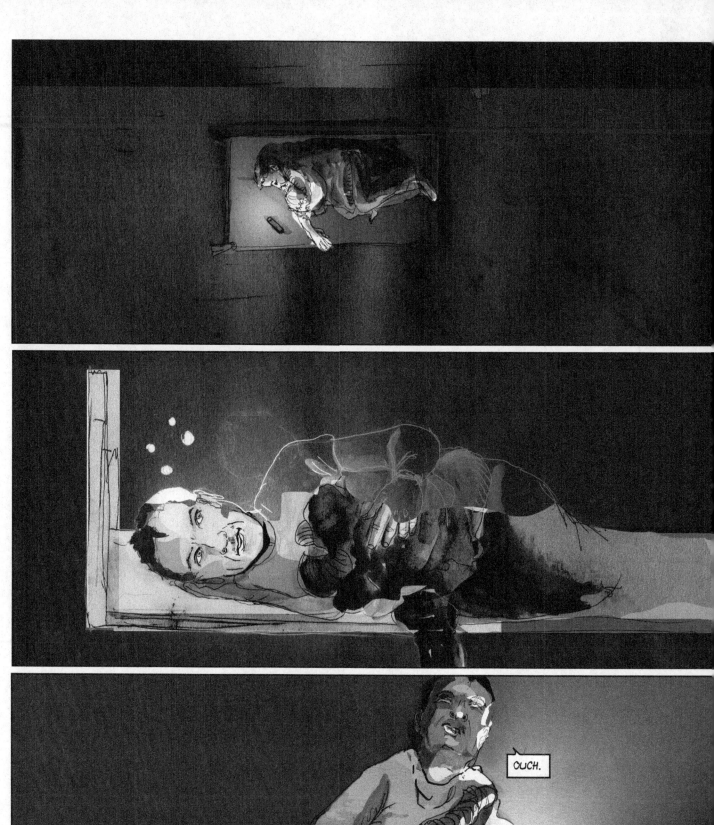
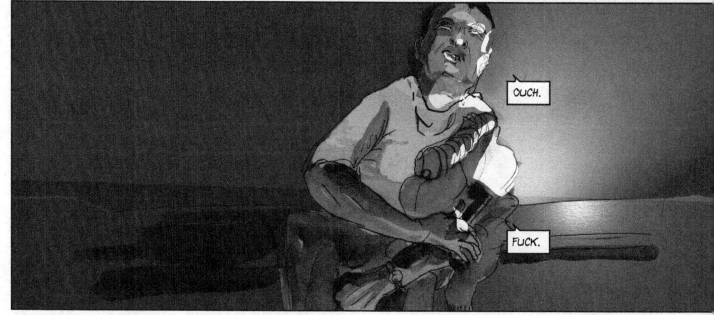

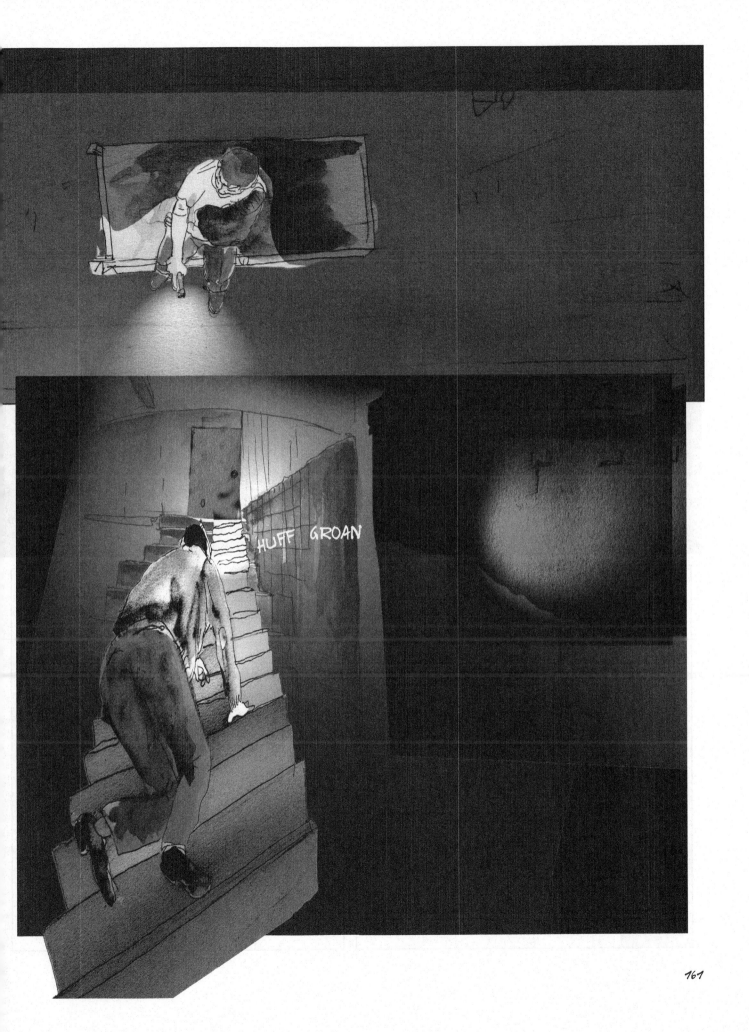

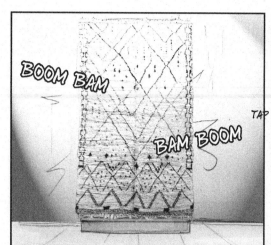

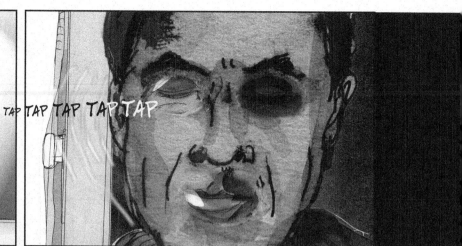

162

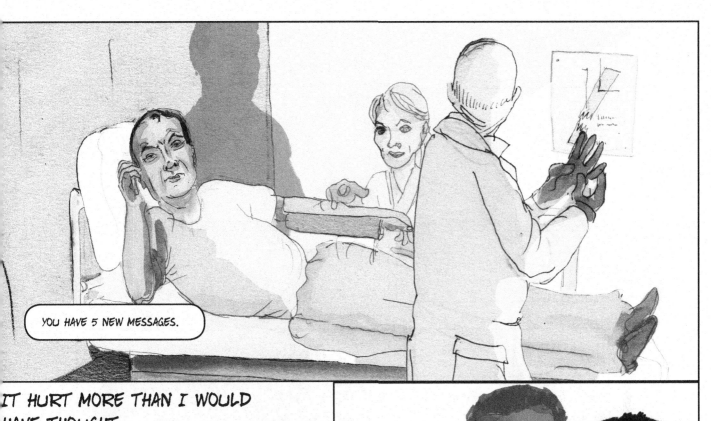

YOU HAVE 5 NEW MESSAGES.

IT HURT MORE THAN I WOULD HAVE THOUGHT.

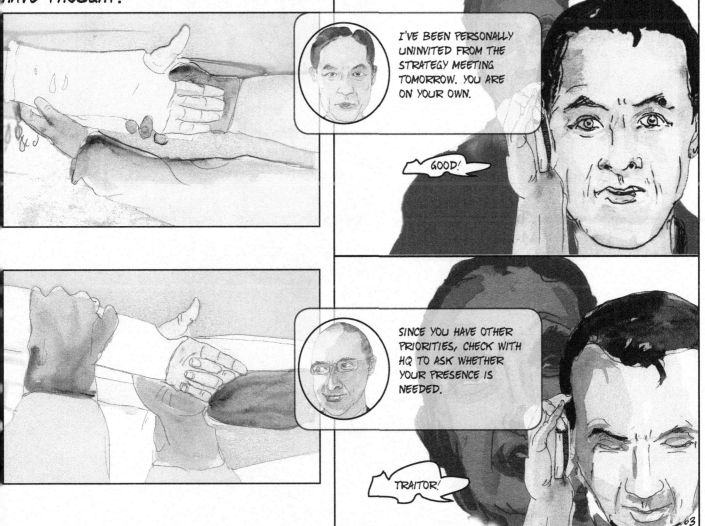

I'VE BEEN PERSONALLY UNINVITED FROM THE STRATEGY MEETING TOMORROW. YOU ARE ON YOUR OWN.

GOOD!

SINCE YOU HAVE OTHER PRIORITIES, CHECK WITH HQ TO ASK WHETHER YOUR PRESENCE IS NEEDED.

TRAITOR!

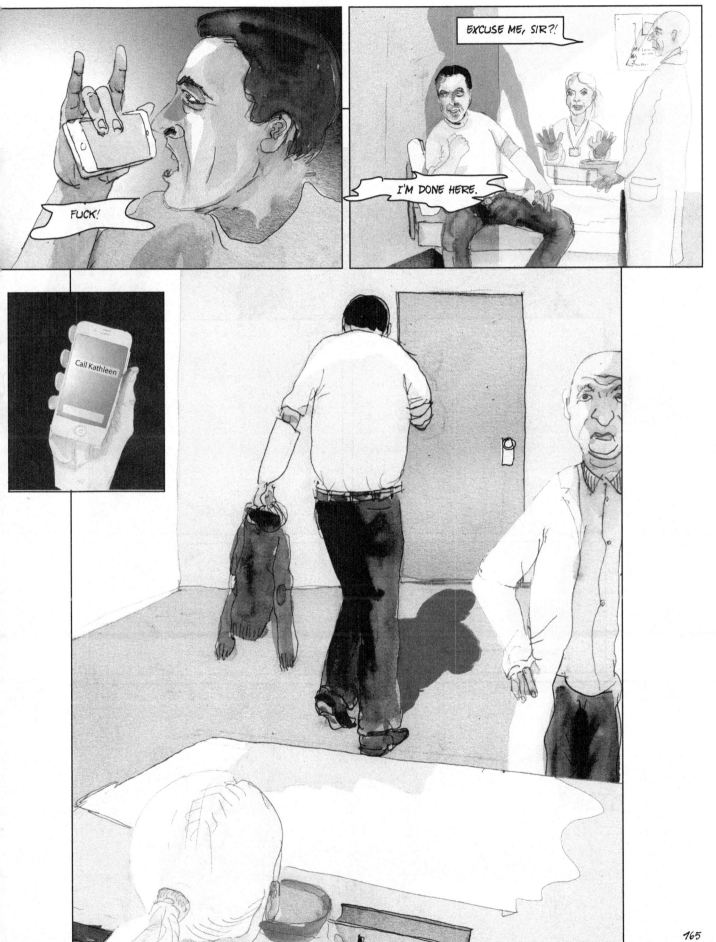

165

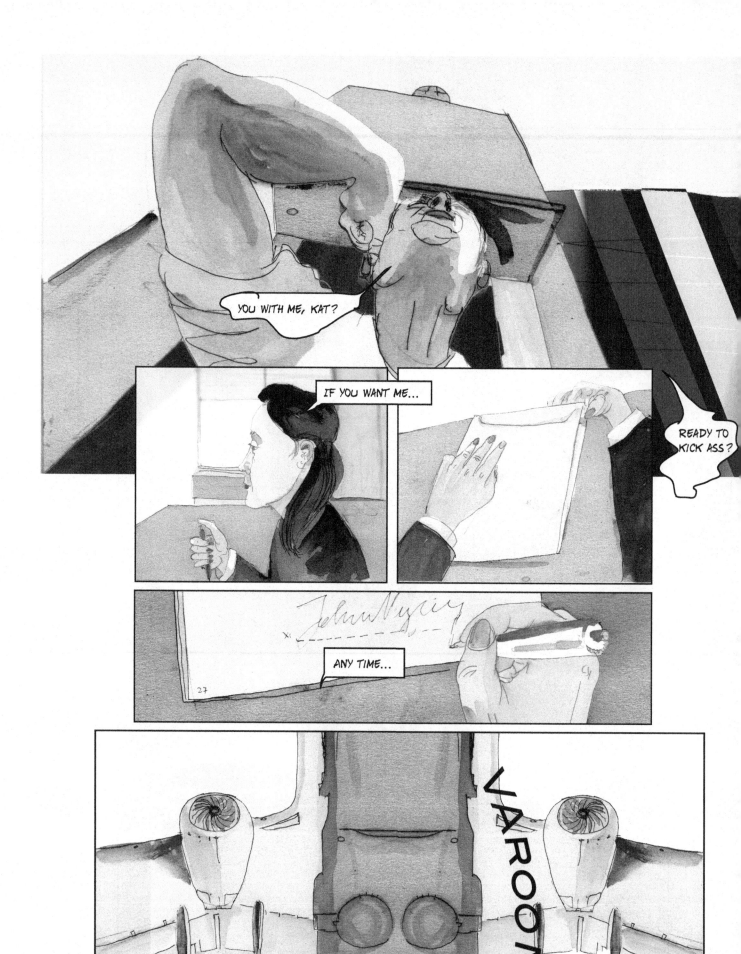

166

TIP TIP TAPATATAP TIP TIP TAP

I FELT LIKE I ALWAYS FEEL WHEN I'M IN CHARGE AND POWERFUL.

BUT SOMETHING HAD CHANGED.

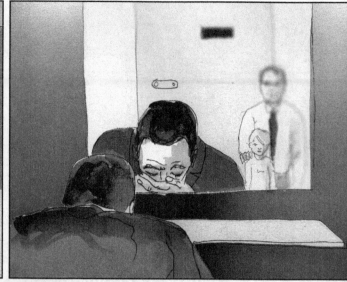

I SAW MYSELF LIKE I'VE NEVER SEEN MYSELF BEFORE.

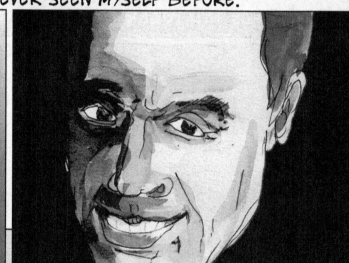

... SO THE INDIAN GOVERNMENT DROPPED SECURITY, HEALTH AND OTHER RESTRICTIONS. WE ARE MOVING IN AND WE'RE ABLE TO REALIZE PROFITS WAY ABOVE PLAN.

OUR COUNTRY HEADS BOLDLY CUT EMPLOYMENT NUMBERS AND SAVED MORE MONEY THAN EXPECTED.

I'M PROUD TO ANNOUNCE THAT DESPITE DIFFICULT MARKETS, WE'RE MARKET LEADER.

OUR TOUGHNESS IS THE BENCHMARK FOR THE WHOLE INDUSTRY.

WE ARE ITWORLD!

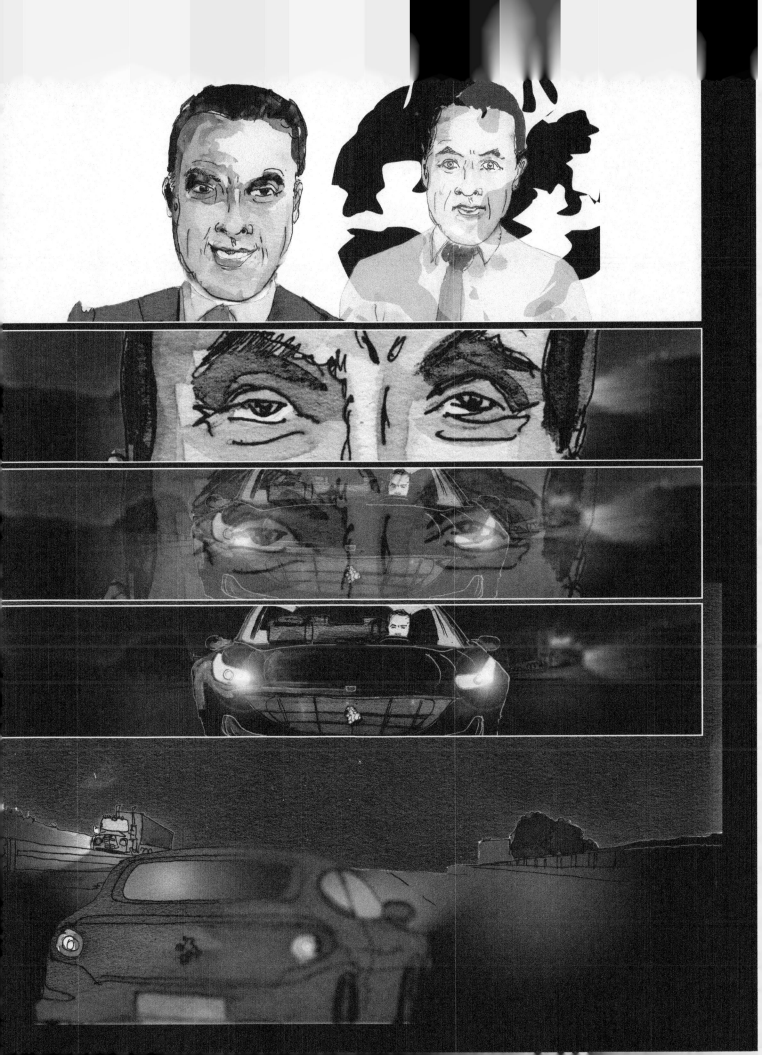

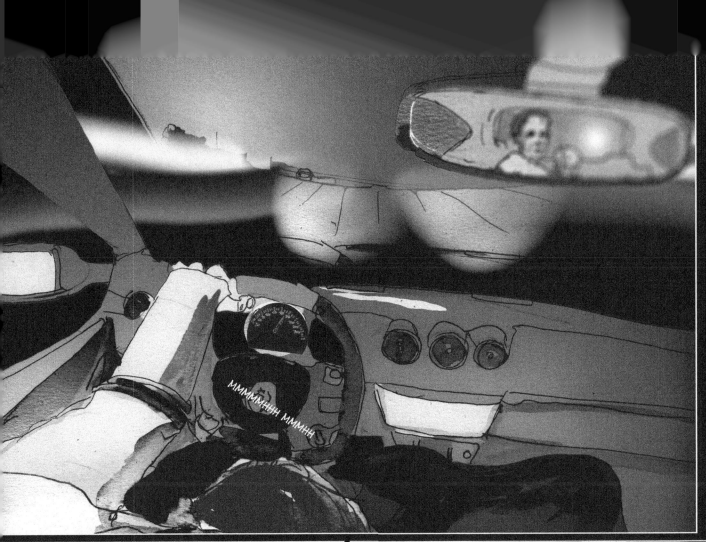

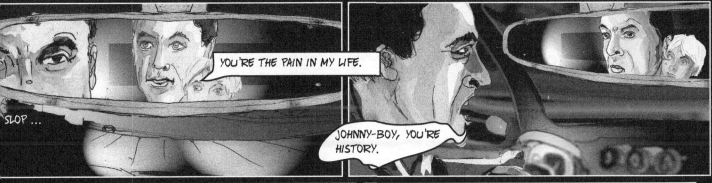

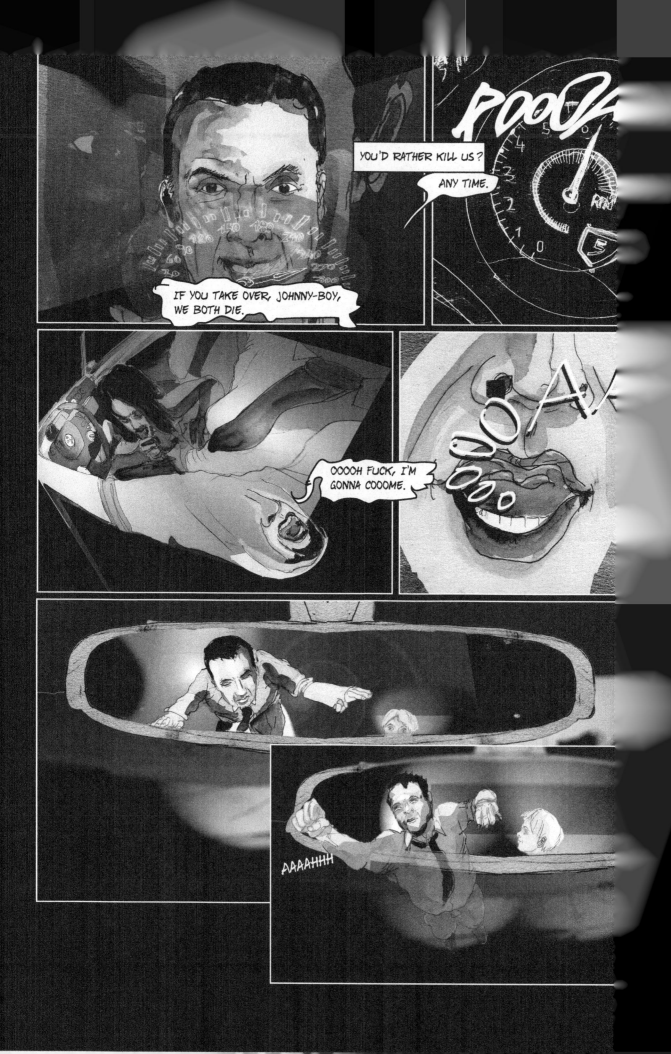

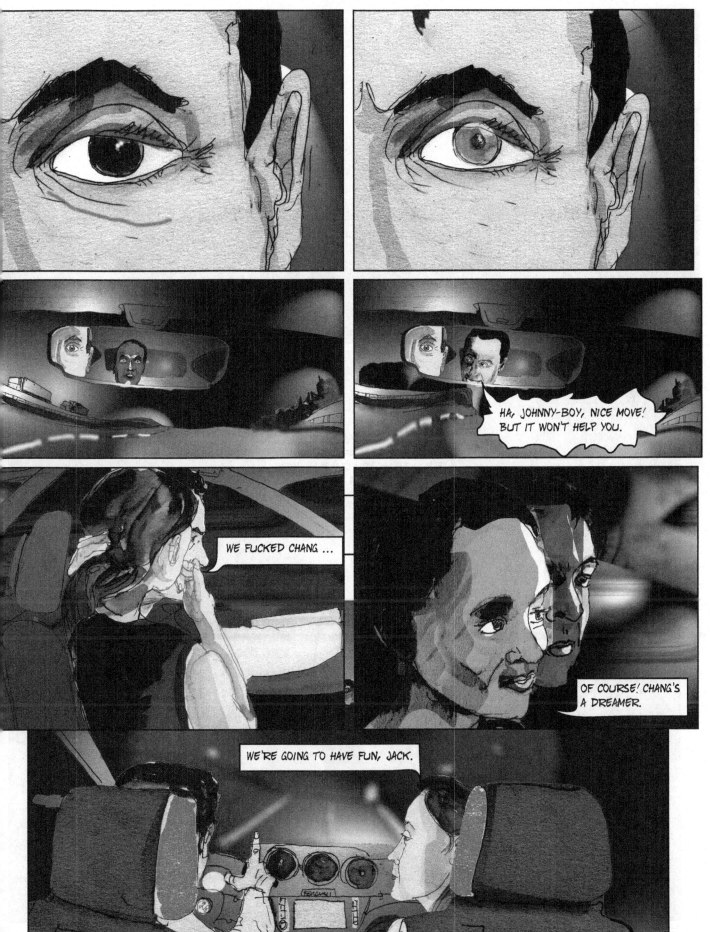

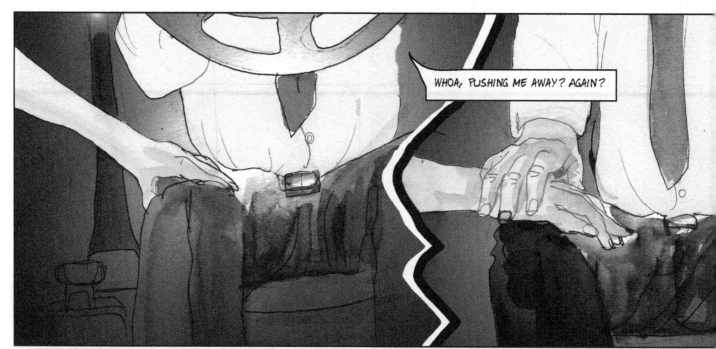

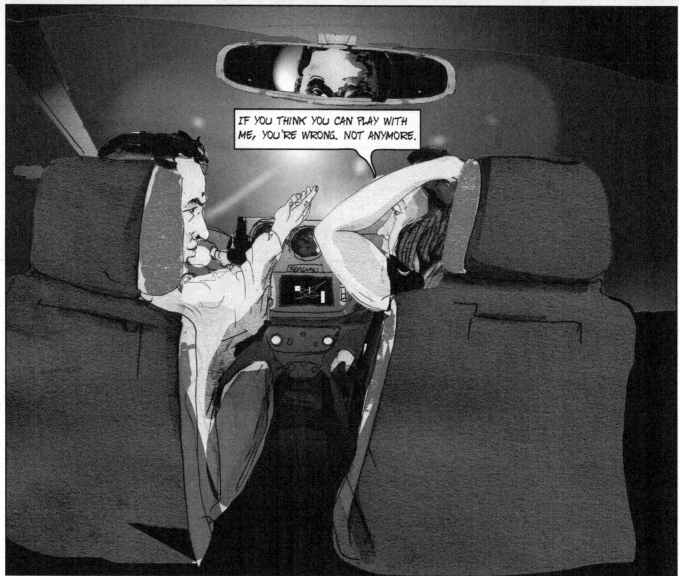

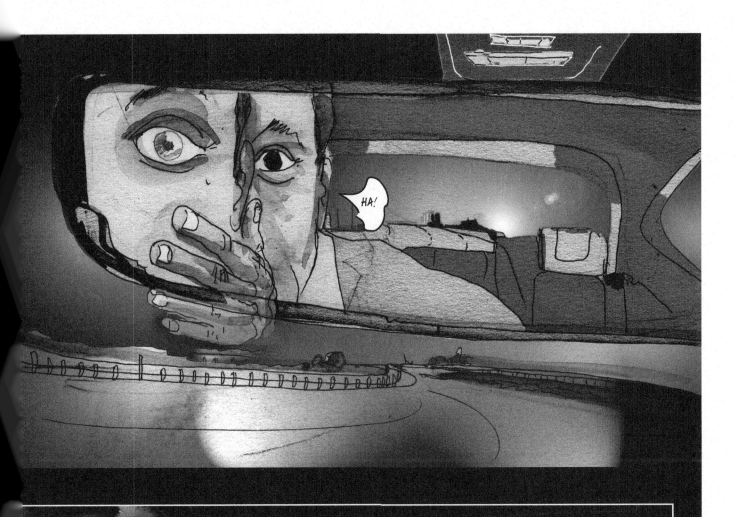

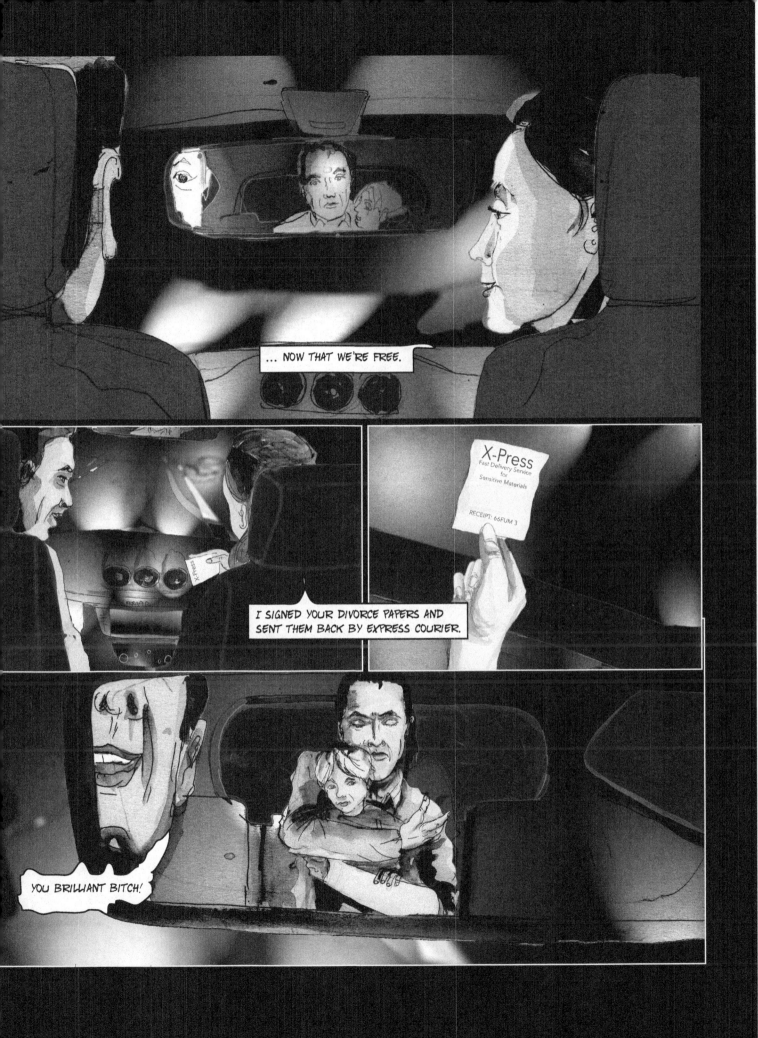

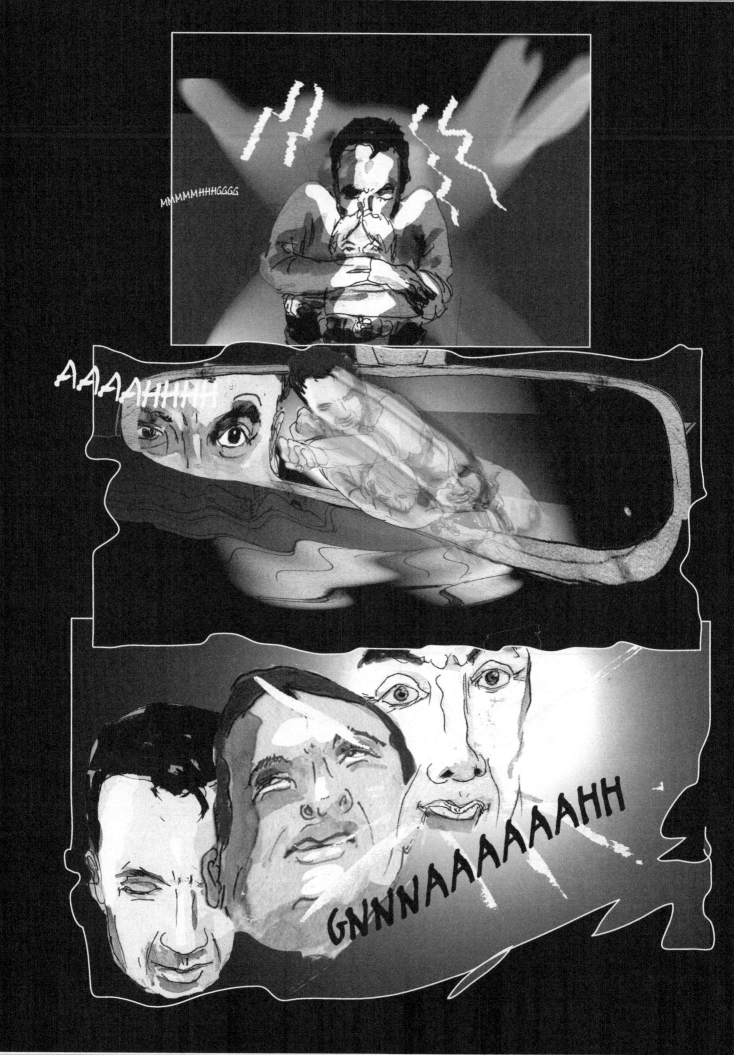

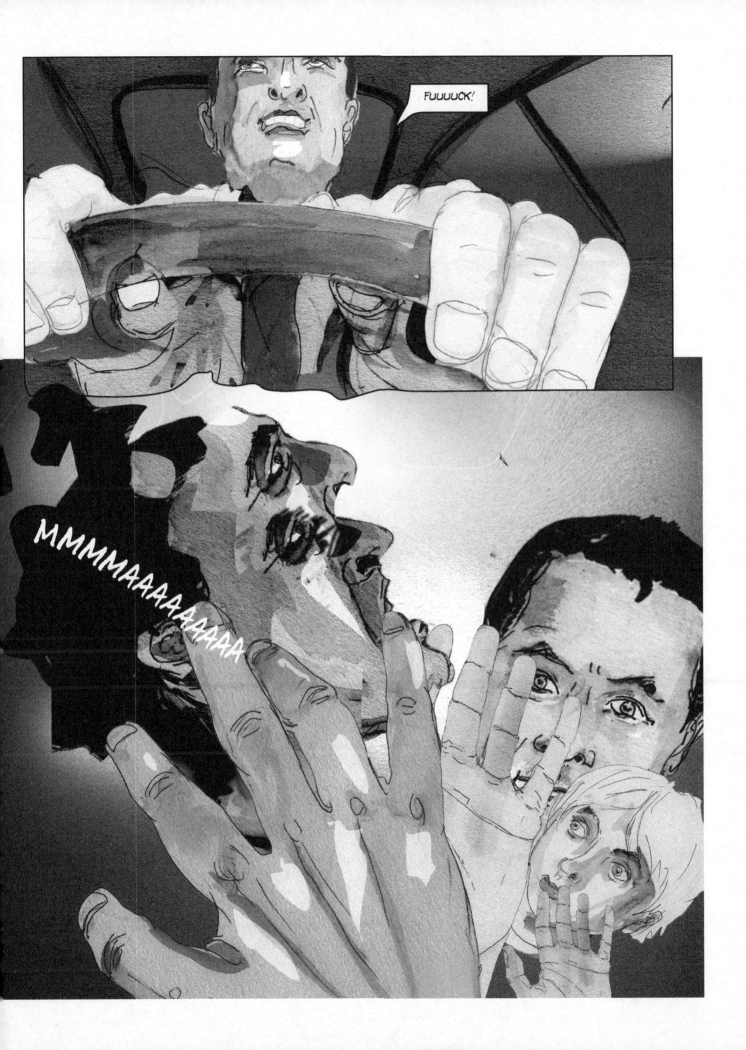

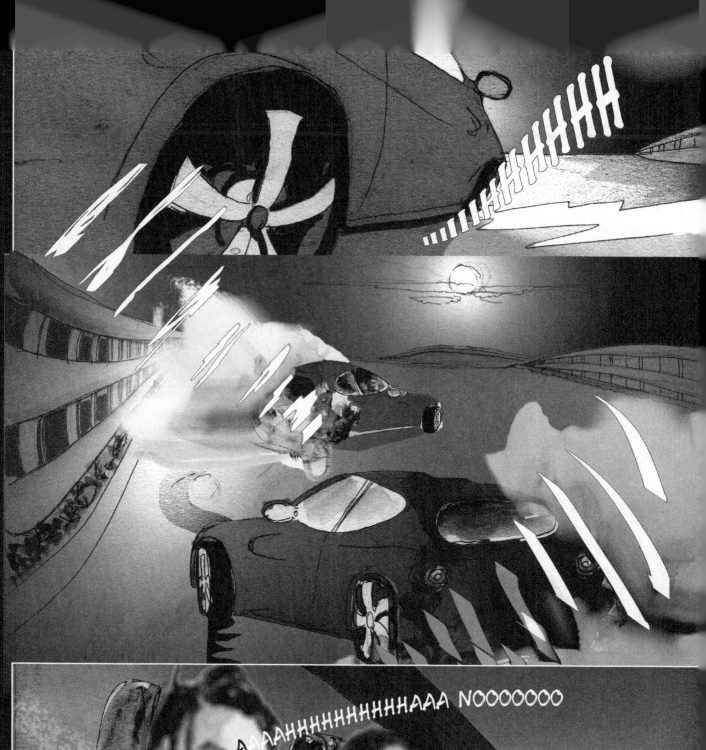

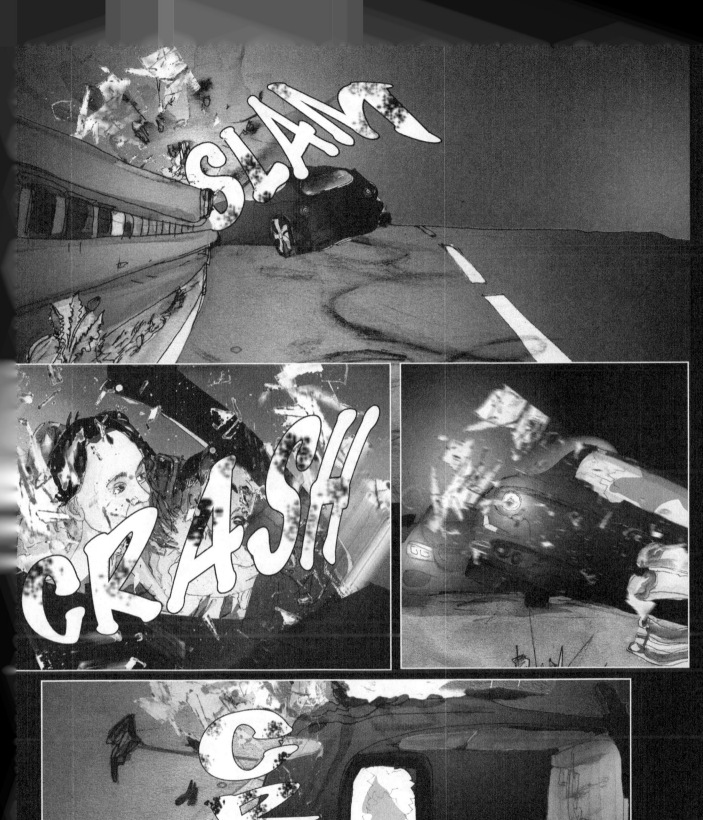

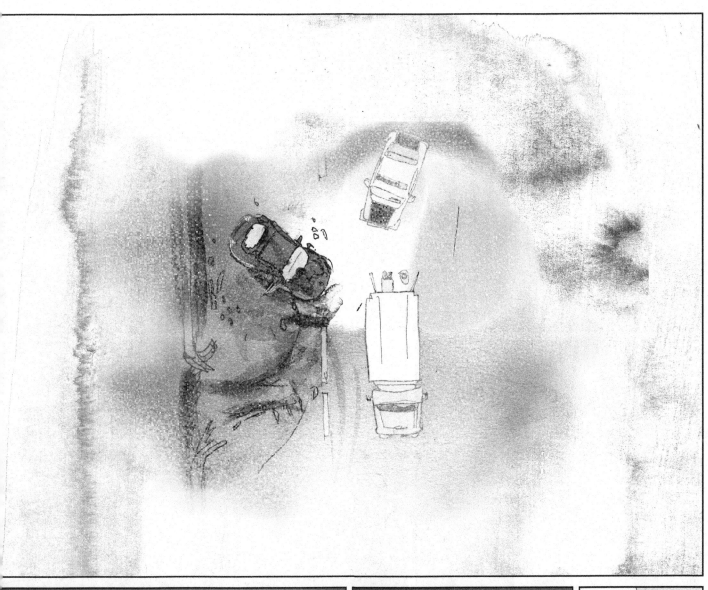

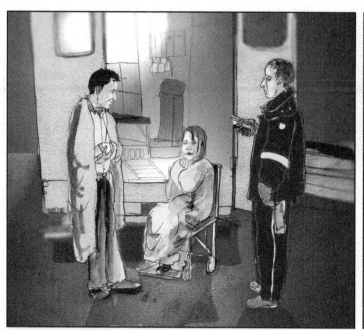

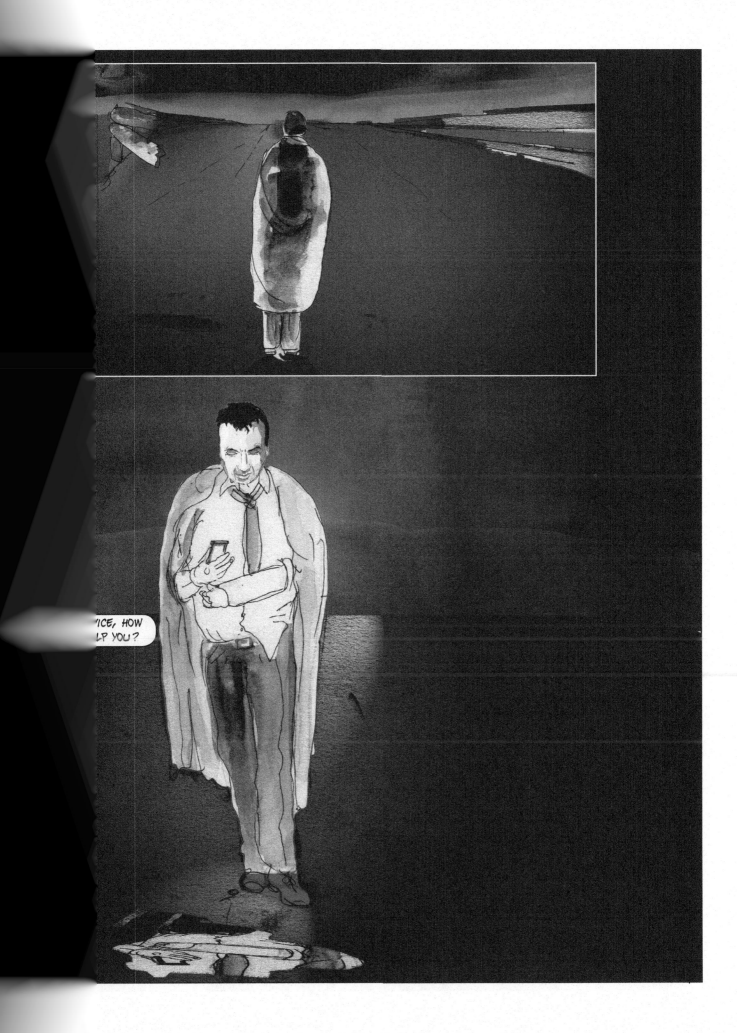

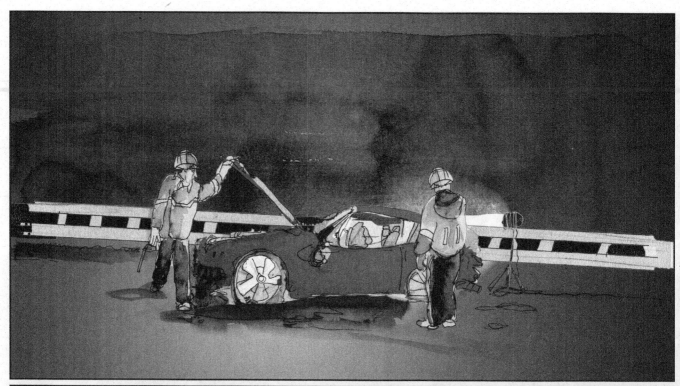